PORK BELLY TACOS
with a Side of Anxiety

by Yvonne Castañeda

SANTA
MONICA
PRESS
TEEN

Published by: Santa Monica Press LLC
P.O. Box 850
Solana Beach, CA 92075
1-800-784-9553
www.santamonicapress.com
books@santamonicapress.com

S A N T A
MONICA
P R E S S
TEEN

Printed in the United States

ISBN-13 978-1-59580-108-1 (print)
ISBN-13 978-1-59580-784-7 (ebook)

Publisher's Cataloging-in-Publication data

Names: Castañeda, Yvonne, author.
Title: Pork belly tacos with a side of anxiety : my journey through depression , bulimia , and addiction / by Yvonne Castañeda.
Description: Solana Beach, CA: Santa Monica Press, 2022.
Identifiers: ISBN: 978-1-59580-108-1 (print) | 978-1-59580-784-7 (ebook)
Subjects: LCSH Castañeda, Yvonne. | Bulimia--Patients--United States--Biography. | Depressed persons--United States--Biography. | Substance abuse--Patients--Biography. | Miami (Fla.)--Biography. | Cuban Americans--Biography. | Mexican Americans--Biography. | Hispanic Americans--Biography. | Self-actualization (Psychology) | BISAC YOUNG ADULT NONFICTION / Biography & Autobiography / Cultural, Ethnic & Regional | YOUNG ADULT NONFICTION / Social Topics / Eating Disorders & Body Image | YOUNG ADULT NONFICTION / Social Topics / Depression & Mental Illness | YOUNG ADULT NONFICTION / Social Topics / Self-Esteem & Self-Reliance | YOUNG ADULT NONFICTION / People & Places / United States / Hispanic & Latino | YOUNG ADULT NONFICTION / Social Topics / Drugs, Alcohol, Substance Abuse
Classification: LCC E184.S75 C37 2022 | DDC 973.0568/092--dc23

Cover and interior design and production by Future Studio

Cover illustration: © Michal Sanca/Dreamstime.com

DEDICATION

To Savannah, Emma, Karina, Nikki, Becca, Jessie,
Andrew, Alessandra, and Alessio.
May you never stray from the truth.

There is a life-force
within your soul,
seek that life.

There is a gem in the
mountain of your body,
seek that mine.

O traveler, if you are
in search of that,
don't look outside,
look inside yourself
and seek That.

—RUMI

CONTENTS

Author's Note 7

1. Toy Piano 9
2. Do I Have to Be a Woman? 23
3. Bull's-eye on My Back 43
4. The Elephant on My Chest 53
5. *Mejico lindo* 67
6. Pom Pom Nightmare 79
7. Legs Too Fat! You Too Fat! 89
8. All Aboard! 103
9. Speed Train to Hell 111
10. Road Tripping 123
11. A Broken Compass 145
12. Keeping Secrets 157
13. My Favorite Mistake 169
14. Only God Knows 193
15. Drifting Away 207
16. Traumatized Tooth Fairy 217
17. Imposter Syndrome 231
18. Single and Badass 245
19. Jumping off the Train 251
20. *La Solución* 257
21. Epilogue 269
    Acknowledgments 276
    Resources 279
    About the Author 280

AUTHOR'S NOTE

I HAD BEEN SITTING ON THE IDEA TO SHARE THIS STORY for many years, and it wasn't until I entered graduate school that I found the courage to articulate my thoughts and feelings on paper, to allow myself to be vulnerable. I feel strongly that when we share our experiences, we give someone an opportunity to see themselves reflected in the pages, and perhaps provide them with the hope and strength they need to find their own path forward.

To say that it was difficult to write this story would be a massive understatement. It was triggering and scary, at times embarrassing and painful. Using words like "fat" and "chubby" to describe myself were a constant reminder that the world in which I grew up was not fully aware of the negative impact words can have on our self-perception. I use these words throughout the book to provide context for the story; however, in no way do I endorse the use of these words today. I am grateful for the way in which we, as a society, have become more mindful of our words, more considerate of others, and more compassionate toward those who suffer from mental illness and addiction. We have a long way to go, but I am hopeful that we are headed in the right direction.

I am mindful that this story may be highly triggering for anyone who is suffering or in recovery from an eating disorder or mental illness, and my hope is that this book will encourage them to make use of the resources provided in the resource section.

Thank you, reader, for honoring my story.

YVONNE CASTAÑEDA

TOY PIANO

"HILDA, ARE YOU SURE YOU WANT TO GO TO SHAKEY'S Pizza? Are you feeling okay? It's after midnight. *Es muy tarde.*"

The weekly poker game had ended, my nine-months-pregnant mother more than satisfied with her winnings as she hobbled to Tio Lionel's car for a midnight pizza run. "Yes," she said, "Don't worry, I'll be fine. *¡Vámonos!*"

They drove away from the house on Gramercy Place in downtown Los Angeles, a sharp pain causing Mami to hunch over in her seat. "*Aaaaayyyyyy,*" she said, her hand dismissing Tia Leya's suggestion that they take her home. "No, *comadre,*" she said. "I'm fine, don't worry. Besides, we're almost there."

My father was sound asleep in their apartment on St. Andrews Place, having tried and failed to get her to come home with him. "No," she'd said, "I'm on a roll! I can't leave the game now. *Ándale,* let me stay, *¿sí?*" Papi had walked home, already accustomed to Mami's maniacal obsession with poker, this love for gambling the only thing to ever get in the way of her duties as a loyal *esposa.*

At Shakey's, Mami ate her pizza and laughed and purposefully hid the pains in her belly, God forbid she ruin the night by opening her mouth and saying something. The pains intensified and came more frequently as the night went on, and she'd bitten her tongue a million times by the time she laid down next to Papi. Unable to contain the pain, her screams pierced the night, causing Papi to shoot out of bed and call Tia Leya. "*Oye,* I think it's time, come with us to the hospital."

Papi drove fast as Mami continued to scream with each sharp pain. She was confused and scared because this delivery was feeling very different from the one she'd had only three years prior when she'd given birth to my brother Raz.

They arrived at French Hospital in Chinatown, Mami barely able to walk but making it to the emergency entrance, their horror palpable as they realized the entrance doors were locked. They screamed and banged on the glass with their palms, alerting the staff to their emergency as Mami's water broke right then and there. Mami was quickly whisked away in a wheelchair and wheeled into a delivery room, where a young doctor was left with no time to prep or shave Mami or even put on gloves because I couldn't wait to come into the world, my little body bursting into the atmosphere, Mami crying as the doctor placed me on her stomach and said, "It's a girl! And clearly she is ready for life!"

Mami would later say the nature of my arrival was a sign, a clear indication that I would grow to be fearless and strong, that I would always be hungry for life and take great measures to satisfy this insatiable appetite, that I would run toward my life rather than away. The story of my birth thus transformed into a self-fulfilling prophecy, my determination to realize this prediction possibly the reason no one considered that perhaps I'd shown up in the world with a sword in one hand and mental vulnerabilities in the other.

Nobody could have known because long before my first day of kindergarten at Dan T. Williams Elementary School, I had been making it known that I could be left alone for long periods of time without so much as a peep for attention or a cry for help. Mami stayed home with me after Raz when to school, her days refreshingly quiet because I was easily amused by any number of things. My little body would bend over and reach into the laundry basket on the floor to grab one of Papi's socks, an item with which I would play for hours while Mami folded Papi's shirts and *calzoncillos*, the TV permanently tuned to PBS because I loved to watch *Sesame Street* and *Villa Alegre*, my brown eyes lost in the colorful images. By three years old, I'd learned to count to one hundred and to say my ABCs in both English and Spanish, my brain primed for learning as Mami counted down the days to kindergarten.

The night before my first day of school, Mami tucked us in and blessed us with the sign of the cross. Too excited to sleep, I overheard Mami talking to Papi in the small kitchen.

"*Ay Dios mío*, I hope she doesn't scream and cry tomorrow like her brother did."

"No, Hilda," Papi said, "I don't think she'll cry. *Ella es muy diferente.*"

"*Ojalá*, but I'm going to pray that she doesn't cry because I don't want to go through that again."

That night, as my brother Raz slept in the other twin bed, I wondered why he'd been afraid to go to school. As far as I knew, it was a place where I would learn more fun things beyond what Bert and Ernie had shown me. "*Mija*, school is very important," Mami had said. "You are going to learn *muchas cosas* and get to play with other little boys and girls just like you."

Mami walked me to school the next morning, my hand in hers as I practically skipped the whole way, a

Hanna- Barbera metal lunchbox in my other hand as we walked down Vandorf Street and across Delmar Avenue, my excitement growing as I saw other little kids being led by their moms into the school. Mami brought me all the way to the kindergarten classroom of Mrs. Luango, a beautiful woman who smiled warmly as she greeted Mami and bent down to say hello to me. "Hello there, what's your name?" Her beautiful Hawaiian eyes twinkled as I told her my name. "It's Yvonne. Are you my teacher?" She nodded and encouraged me to find somewhere to sit.

Without hesitation, I let go of Mami's hand and proceeded to find a seat, my joy at being with other little boys and girls so great that I forgot to say goodbye to Mami, who was standing in the doorway with tears streaming down her face.

"Yvonne," she said, loud enough to get my attention, "*ya me voy*. I'm leaving now, okay?"

I stayed in my little wooden chair and waved at her. "Okay, Mami! You can leave! But don't cry, I'm not scared!"

Mami wiped her eyes and blew me a kiss. "I'll pick you up later, okay?"

"*Sí*, Mami, okay. Bye!"

Mami would leave that day and wonder at the differences between me and Raz, at the easy way I embraced the unknown and dove headfirst into things about which I knew nothing.

We did not have a life of luxury. Our humble home instead was rich in emotion, with hugs and *besitos* a regular occurrence. Having been extremely poor as children, my parents' first-hand experiences with poverty fueled their desire to give us what they'd never had, namely food. Mami mended a scraped knee with a butterfly Band-Aid, a kiss on the forehead, and a huge bowl of strawberry ice cream; she soothed my fears after a nightmare with a big glass of ice cold *chocomil*, a Mexican version of chocolate milk.

Dinner time at the Castañeda house was a spread of calorie dense foods: beans and rice, breaded steak and *tostones* or *platanos maduros, pastelitos de guayaba* for dessert. Mami piled food on our plates and made sure we consumed every last morsel before we got up from the table.

Dinner aside, Mami let us eat whatever we wanted, no matter the time of day. "Mami, can I have a donut?" I'd say as she tucked me into bed. "*Sí.* Which one? ¿*El chocolate*?" She'd return with the chocolate donut and a glass of milk, her face awash with love as she waited for me to finish eating, insistent on blessing me with the sign of the cross to ward off nightmares when what I needed was a blessing to ward off excess fat.

Access to food and loving parents provided me with a healthy foundation on which both my spirit and body could grow, the rapid physical expansion of my body exacerbated by a surprise talent for piano that pretty much guaranteed I'd never spend hours playing a sport, a nightmare come true for my older brother.

We were at Toys R Us, Papi having given me the chance to choose one toy for my fourth birthday, Raz's dream of turning me into a professional athlete/criminal coming to an end as I looked at dollhouses and Barbies. Raz had been trying to turn me into a little brother for years, someone with whom he could play sports and wrestle. How to throw a football, hit a baseball, and kick a soccer ball *like a boy* had been part of our daily lessons during which I'd sworn allegiance to The Dallas Cowboys and promised to never never close my eyes when I swung the baseball bat. His dream for me was that I learn to set random objects on fire, tackle someone like a boss, and catch lizards with my bare hands, not walk around Toys R Us looking at dolls and girl stuff.

We walked the aisles of our favorite store, my eyes searching for that one special toy as Raz tried to talk me into getting green Army men. My chubby legs came to a halt when my brown eyes landed on a toy piano, the colorful keys and tiny bench drawing me in to take a closer look, the picture on the box of a little girl with yellow hair smiling from ear to ear causing my heart to flutter.

I pointed to the box, excitement in my voice. "*Eso,*" I said. "*Eso,* Papi. *Eso.*"

Raz rolled his eyes as Papi looked at the toy piano, logically surprised because nobody in our family played an instrument. "This is what you want?" Papi said. "¿*Un piano?*"

"Uh-huh, *sí.*"

"Are you sure you're going to play it? ¿*Eh?*"

"*Sí, Papi,* I promise."

He smiled. "*Bueno.*" He grabbed the box off the shelf.

Excitedly, I hopped up and down, all other toy options forgotten as I followed Papi to the register. So afraid to be separated from my new toy, I insisted on sitting in the back seat with the big box on top of my small legs, my arms hugging my new treasure as Papi drove us home.

True to my word, I played my toy piano for hours on end, the beautiful sounds provoked by my fingers filling me with unbelievable joy. With as much passion as I could muster at the age of four, I played "Twinkle, Twinkle, Little Star" and "Mary Had a Little Lamb," and held mock recitals for the dolls that I positioned on the floor in front of the piano. I played for whoever would listen: my Tio Abel or Tio Mario or Tio Jaime or Tio Luis, uncles who'd left Mexico and slipped into the US unnoticed, their moustaches spreading wide across their brown faces as they smiled. "*Órale, mija,* you're so talented." I played for my Tia Esperanza, Mami's sister, and any one of her six children; Veronica or Bobby or Adrian or Fabian or Marcos or Armandito, cousins with whom we spent a great deal of time.

I gravitated to pianos that did not belong to me, like the one in my Tia Leya's apartment. While Raz and my cousins Jorge, Osiris, Odalys, and Ana played Monopoly or Life, my tiny hands would press the ivory keys for hours, my legs swinging back and forth as I played the songs I knew well and songs I tried to create myself.

Eventually, my body's vertical and horizontal growth would make it impossible to sit on the tiny bench of my toy piano, my face sad as Mami put it away and encouraged me to play with Dawn, the little girl who lived next door with her large American family. Dawn and I became best friends in a matter of seconds, our laughter filling the air as daily we played with our Weebles Haunted House or rode our bikes or played in the small plastic pool that Papi bought for us each year. Wanting all the Mexican kids in the neighborhood to experience the fun of camping, Dawn's father set up a large tent in their backyard and invited us to bring our sleeping bags, our faces smiling as we munched on S'mores that were somehow made without a real campfire.

Surrounded by so much family and having found a best friend in Dawn, it was easy to forget about my love for piano, even more so after Mami told me we were going on a long vacation shortly after I turned seven.

"Where are we going?"

Mami was tucking me in, her eyes sad. "We're going to drive far away, *mija*."

"To Tijuana? To Ensenada? To that hotel with the pool on the second floor?"

"No, *mija*, somewhere else."

"Are we going with everyone? With Tio Armando and Tia Esperanza and *mis primos*?"

She shook her head. "No, not this time." Her eyes filled with tears even as she smiled, which confused me. I couldn't understand why a vacation would make Mami cry. "This time we are going alone. *Ándale*, go to sleep."

She turned out the light and shut the door, leaving me alone to ask Jesus to help us find a motel near the beach, one with a pool like the one at the Motel Presidente in Ensenada, where my older cousin Veronica played with me and always made sure the bigger kids didn't drown me.

Our *vacation* prompted a yard sale on a sunny, Saturday afternoon during which we would be able to rid the house of junk, including my little piano. My heart broke as I watched a girl with two pigtails make off with my favorite toy, my sadness immediately mollified by the *paleta de fresa* Mami handed me, her soothing voice reminding me that my Holly Hobby Easy Bake Oven would be coming with us on the vacation, and *si Dios quiere*, someday I would have a real piano.

Early one morning in November, we piled into the red Chevy Caprice Classic and headed down Vandorf Street for the last time, the emptiness of our house and the SOLD sign on the front lawn not able to stop me from believing that we were headed for an adventure, a week-long road trip that would culminate in Miami on Thanksgiving Day, 1978. The idea that we were on vacation faded fast as we temporarily moved into a roach-infested apartment on Bird Road, but the realization that we'd left California for good was not enough to quell my excitement over being enrolled at Tropical Elementary School.

Crammed into a tiny apartment for the first few months, Raz and I fought on a daily basis, putting Papi's temper to the test, whatever stress he felt kept under wraps as we argued over board games like Risk or Life. On the one occasion that Papi's anger got the best of him, he got up from the couch and walked over to where we were sitting on the floor, bent over and picked up the Monopoly board over which we were fighting, and ripped it to pieces, his breathing labored as he put everything inside a black garbage bag and walked out the door.

Shocked to see Papi do anything in anger, Raz and I looked at each other, the fear we both felt creating a temporary bond and forcing us to get along for ten minutes, during which we waited for Papi to walk back in the door and hit us. Yet Papi was the picture of calm when he returned, the smell of cigarettes strong as he sat back down on the couch and continued to watch his TV program.

Not a word was said, not even when Papi came home the next day with a brand-new Monopoly game, his way of apologizing for being angry.

We were all happy to move out of the apartment and into our new home. Papi beamed with more pride than a Cuban flag as the realtor handed him the keys. He'd landed a good job working construction that paid enough for a four-bedroom house in Westwood Lakes, a working-class neighborhood in the southwest part of greater Miami. The house seemed enormous to us, what with the living room *and* Florida room, two bathrooms and a large backyard with various fruit bearing trees: mango, lemon, orange, avocado.

My toy piano lost to me forever, I was not prepared for the sight of an upright piano in the living room. My eyes grew wide in disbelief as I inched my way toward it. I turned to look at Mami and Papi, their smiles an indicator that this was no mistake, the reddish-brown Kimball was a gift for me, an act of kindness from the family who'd sold us the home, their gesture delivered with strings attached: "Please don't let it go to waste, Mr. Castañeda."

Soon after we settled in, Papi and Mami began their search for a piano teacher in the Dark Ages version of Google: The Yellow Pages. With no Yelp reviews to guide them, they settled on the first teacher with a Latino name, her teaching experience irrelevant because Papi cared more that I'd be learning from *una Cubana,* a fact that more than pleased him because in his not-so-humble opinion, Cubans were the best at everything.

Mrs. Romero and her dark, bushy eyebrows scared the hell out of me, the large mole just above her lip a distraction as she yelled at me to follow the metronome, *tick tock tick tock tick tock;* her horrible breath on my face making me nauseated as she hit my hands with a ruler and told me to "Sit up straight, *¡coño!*" No surprise, I began to dread my weekly lesson, my love for piano not strong enough to withstand the pain I felt each time she smacked my little hands.

Mami was my biggest fan, and when I told her Mrs. Romero was downright mean, she believed me. I wondered if Mami would tell Mrs. Romero the truth about why I didn't want to return, but Mami thanked her for her time and then lied. "Yvonne has decided to quit piano lessons," she said into the phone. "*Es que* she has a lot of homework." Mami's lying scared me because I worried about her chances of going to heaven and meeting Jesus, Catholicism having taught me that lying was *un pecado,* a sin. Besides, rather than quit piano, I'd quit Mrs. Romero, and that was totally different.

Luckily, Papi had a friend from Cuba who'd moved to Miami with his own family years before, and he recommended the piano teacher with whom his own daughter was taking lessons, an idea that Papi liked so much better than resorting to the Yellow Pages.

A spicy *Cubana* who lived with her son and husband in a tiny apartment in Little Havana just off *Calle Ocho,* Martha Moreno was a force of nature, a storm of energy and passion that immediately drew me in rather than scare me away. She left Cuba in the early 1960s and like Papi, she was a proud Cuban. All around her tiny apartment were reminders of her *patria*: a Cuban flag in the tiny kitchen, a picture of Havana just above the couch, a statue of *La Santa Barbara* way too big for the side table on which it was placed. For the first few lessons, I braced myself for the inevitable ruler, my fears alleviated by the presence of Mami on the couch, by the soothing *tick tock* of the metronome, and by the nice minty quality of Martha's breath as she leaned across me to turn the page.

Martha introduced me to Beethoven, Chopin, Mozart, Rachmaninoff, and Bach, classical composers who challenged me daily, my little fingers often struggling to stretch an octave. A devoted fan of Ernesto Lecuona, a

Cuban composer and pianist, Martha focused many of our lessons on teaching me to play his music, powerful pieces like "Malagueña" or "San Francisco El Grande."

Weekly lessons were a regular thing for all of my childhood and into adolescence, these hour-long visits with Martha Moreno a dedicated effort to develop and hone my talent, one that would lead to a dramatic increase in my overall size as a human being.

Basically, I got fat.

Mami would take me to McDonald's or Burger King for a treat after each lesson, as though she feared my talent would vanish unless I ate a Big Mac, but these treats were full-blown meals, my Big Mac or Whopper always coupled with French fries, a Coke, *and* a hot fudge sundae. No surprise, I looked forward to my piano lessons and the three thousand-plus calories I consumed right before dinner.

My piano skills and body weight developed at lightning speed; my clothes shrank and my cheeks ballooned seemingly overnight. So proud of their super talented *hija*, Mami and Papi said nothing about my rapidly growing body, but my extended family members insured my weight gain didn't escape their attention, God forbid I develop any self-esteem.

"*Oye, la niña* is gaining a lot of weight," my aunt said to Mami, not caring that I was standing right in front of her. "*Está muy gorda.*"

"It's just baby fat," Mami said with conviction. "She'll lose all of it when she gets to puberty."

As though baby fat was a loose tooth that would eventually fall out of my mouth.

Even so, it didn't occur to me that being *gordita* was

an issue; I was too young to wrap my head around the concept because nobody picked on me or bullied me in elementary school, thank God. Even Raz, with whom I argued on a daily basis, never played the "You're so fat" card, perhaps sensing that it had no impact on me and was therefore not worth the effort.

With piano as my primary focus of attention, I continued to eat chocolate donuts at bedtime and mindlessly consume a whole bag of Doritos while I worked on my homework, all the while basking in the praise and attention showered on me for being a child prodigy and a straight A student. All of it combined led me to believe I was special, a belief that vanished the second I hit puberty.

DO I HAVE TO BE A WOMAN?

MY MOM, OR MAMI, IS COMPASSIONATE, KIND, AND OFTEN hilariously quirky. Like many Latina women across generations, she was raised to be of service to others and was taught to put everyone else first—especially her children and husband. Born and raised in Guadalajara, Mexico, Mami is the third oldest of eighteen siblings because television, social media, and birth control did not exist in rural Mexico circa 1920. She helped to raise many of her siblings in a poverty-stricken environment, and she spent most of her formative years cooking, cleaning, and doing laundry, never stopping to question why she never got to play or make friends.

Mami had not the time nor the headspace to explore her interests, to develop life goals, or to dream beyond the confines of poverty in which she lived, her mindset instead rooted in the here and now, in fear and the struggle to survive: "What are we going to eat today? How are we going to survive?" This unrelenting fear gave birth to an admirable level of resilience that she credits not to her own strength, but to her enduring faith in God, never one to accept praise for everything she has accomplished on her own.

Mami is a warrior, the ultimate solution finder, the redeemer, my "Give it to me and I will fix it" person. Her ability to persevere was the reason Mami always found a way to make things work, obstacles be damned.

One such example finds me at five years old, a smile on my face, my hand in Mami's as we leave the Starlite Swap Meet in Rosemead, California, her hand gripping mine a little harder as she says, *"No me sueltes la mano, mija."* I nod because I would never dream of letting go, not when she'd just bought me a new raincoat with matching boots and an umbrella, the matching set an explosion of pink, purple, and yellow flowers. I couldn't wait to wear my new outfit, but my chances were limited in sunny Southern California.

For days I stared out the window, hoping the beautiful skies would cloud over and deliver rain. "*¿Va llover hoy?*" I would ask.

"Not today, *mija*," Mami would say. "Maybe tomorrow." Tomorrow would come and with it more sunshine and blue skies.

Mami found me kneeling on the couch one day, my body facing the window, eyes closed and prayer hands on my chest. "Dear Jesus, please can you make it rain today, just for five minutes. I promise I will be good for the rest of my whole long life, Amen."

She tapped me on the shoulder, startling me. "*¡ándale!*" she said with urgency. "Hurry up! Put on your raincoat, the boots, and grab the umbrella! *¡Vámonos!*" I jumped off the couch and ran to my bedroom. *Jesus works fast,* I thought.

Plastic umbrella in my hand, I followed Mami out the back door of the house, where she led me down the steps and into the yard. "Open the umbrella," she said, as she grabbed the water hose and turned on the water.

Shading my eyes, I looked up and all around. "*Pero* it's not raining, Mami," I said.

She scoffed. "*¿Ah, no? Pues*, you'll see." Water hose in hand, she walked back up to the top of the stairs. "*A ver, mija*, stand right here," she pointed. "*Aquí nomás*, at the edge of the stairs!" Not used to walking in rainboots, I shuffled like a newborn penguin. "Close your eyes, and don't open them until you hear the rain, *¡ándale!*"

I stood under my plastic umbrella and closed my eyes, opening them only when I heard the sound of water hitting the umbrella. I giggled, excited about the makeshift rain shower, the purple and pink flowers of my umbrella catching the rays of the sun and the droplets of water at the same time. Mami yelled at me to walk around so I could get use of my boots, the stream of water following me as I walked around. From then on, I believed Mami had magical powers, that she could solve every single one of my problems.

Mami is the epitome of selflessness, a woman who represents the meaning of hard work, dedication, and sacrifice. But sweet Jesus, she is a nervous wreck.

Mami has always relied on signs from God and messages from heaven that manifest as intuition or vivid dreams, both of which dictate her feelings. When she gets a *feeling* something terrible might happen, "*Tengo un presentimiento,*" she wrings her hands and talks to herself as she paces back and forth. Her forehead creases with worry and no amount of *té de manzanilla* will calm her down. She refers to this distress as her *nervios*, i.e. anxiety, a word that we heard often throughout our childhood, this expression a way for Mami to let us know the rapture was imminent.

Raz and I would be sitting at the dining room table, crayons and coloring books keeping us busy, while Mami paced around the kitchen, hands clasped and eyes on the floor as though linoleum was to blame for her distress. "*Ay Dios mío, tengo los nervios a millón.*"

"Uh-oh," Raz would say as he grabbed the blue crayon. "Mami's nerves are going a thousand miles an hour."

"Did we do something wrong?" I'd say.

Too focused on coloring, Raz would shrug. I'd rush to finish my masterpiece and run over to show Mami, her smile the reassurance I needed to let me know the world was not ending.

Sitting in front of the television, Raz and I engrossed in *Mister Roger's Neighborhood*, Mami would pace back and forth behind the couch, her head shaking from side to side, her eyes on the floor as though frustrated with our ratty carpet. "*Válgame Dios, estos nervios me quieren matar.*"

"Mami's nerves want to kill her," I'd say to Raz. "What should we do?"

Another shrug. "I don't know. Maybe we should ask Mister Rogers." But Mister Rogers and his red sweater never had an answer.

Papi was laid off from his construction job shortly after I finished the sixth grade, causing Mami's *nervios* to reach a new level of distress, which she communicated to the world in whispers under her breath, "*Bendito sea Dios,* what are we doing to do?" I was playing with my Barbies in the room next to theirs when I overheard my parents talking about it, Mami's near-hysteria filtering through the thin walls of their bedroom.

"Hilda, *tranquila*, we'll figure it out. I'll find work, don't worry."

"A friend at work told me we should apply for food coupons. *¿Qué piensas?*" Mami said, pacing back and forth, her voice traveling from one end of the room to another.

"*Bueno, está bien*, but I don't think we'll need them."

"What if we stop *la niña's* piano lessons for now?"

"*¡No! Eso nunca.*"

"But what if we run out of money?"

"*Coño,* Hilda, *cálmate.* It's going to be okay. *Deja la drama.*" It was the first time I heard Papi raise his voice to Mami, a signal to me that things were not *bueno.*

In spite of Papi's calm, Mami couldn't stop worrying, and failed to mask the concern on her face whenever she found Papi in the kitchen making *cafecito* in the middle of the day. Had she found Papi doing the dishes or helping with laundry, her *nervios* might never have recovered, our culture having determined that Papi's role was man of the house, *el hombre de la casa,* the one who worked to make sure we had food, shelter, and clothing, not the one who did household chores.

I was thrilled that Papi was home and took it upon myself to offer help, hoping it would smooth the worry lines on Mami's forehead.

"Papi, are you going to mow the lawn? I can help."

"*Sí, mija*, maybe later today."

"Papi, are you going to the store? I can come with you."

"*Sí, mija*, in a little while."

Papi remained impressively calm whenever we shopped for toilet paper and mangos, but the petty arguments at the dinner table between me and Raz would sometimes set him off, his sudden outbursts and colloquialisms an indicator that maybe he too had troublesome *nervios.*

"*¡Coño!*" Papi would say. "*¡Me están encendiendo el hígado!*"

"Stop it," Raz would giggle. "We're setting Papi's liver

on fire."

"*¡Me están revolviendo la comida!*" Papi would shout.

"Now we've done it," I'd say. "We're mixing up his food."

Papi would later feel bad for losing his cool, and he'd make it up to all of us by letting us choose what to watch on television.

One day, after I'd helped Papi do yardwork, we sat down at the kitchen table to eat the ham and cheese sandwiches Mami made for us.

"Papi," I asked in between bites, "do you wish you were rich?"

Papi took a sip of his beer. "*¿Qué?* What do you mean? I *am* rich, *mija*."

"Nuh-uh, you're not rich," I said. "We don't have new cars, and we get our clothes at Kmart and the flea market, and Mami said we need food coupons."

Cool as a cucumber, Papi looked me in the eye and said, "*Mija*, I am so rich. Very, very rich!"

I giggled. "You're crazy, Papi."

"No, it's true, *soy rico*, and you know why? *Porque* I wake up every day, have breath in my lungs and *mi familia* is together. *¿Me oíste?* I am rich, *mija*." He put his sandwich down for a moment and looked at me. "So long as you are alive and you have family, you are rich, eh? Don't ever forget that." He winked. "*Anda*, eat your sandwich."

Papi clearly had better control over his *nervios*, but Mami's were a force of nature, an intermittent phenomenon controlled only by certain activities and external factors. During my piano lessons, she would sit on the sofa with her word search puzzles, content to circle words for two hours, her *nervios* lost in an alphabet coma. Each time

I gave her a straight A report card, Mami's face would light up like a Christmas tree—"*Ay mija*, I am so proud of you."—her *nervios* safely buried underneath my accomplishments. Keeping my bedroom clean and not fighting with Raz helped her *nervios* a whole bunch, as did finishing my dinner, taking a bath, showing my teachers respect, and being courteous and polite to adults, regardless of who they were.

Knowing that I could on some level contribute to Mami's sense of calm, I focused all of my efforts on being absolutely perfect, this pressure to be flawless in every area of my life thus triggering my own stupid *nervios*.

A mistake during piano lesson or practice time scared me; I worked that much harder to perfect each piece of music, my palms sweating and heart racing the minute I struck a wrong note or struggled the slightest bit, the shame of it turning my face bright red. Martha would place her hands over mine and tell me to take a deep breath, which worked never, the concern on Mami's face causing me to panic as I quickly tried to repair the tiny mistake I'd made. To calm me down, Martha would offer me a piece of candy or remind me to take a sip of my Coke, but that just made me fatter.

At home, Papi would sometimes sit on the sofa as I practiced, making it difficult to play with abandon because he was the reason I had a piano in the first place and mistakes were criminal. I started to practice before he got home from work, and on weekends, I'd wait until he was outside doing yard work.

Overwhelmed with the pressure to master Beethoven's "Sonata Pathétique," I'd turn to the one thing that always calmed me down: food. I'd step away from the piano to grab a giant bag of Doritos or eat two scoops of Farm Stores chocolate ice cream; a *pastelito de queso y guayaba* or a donut alleviated my fears of not being able to conquer Rachmaninoff.

Getting good grades was of the utmost importance, so I did everything in my power to garner my teachers' love and praise, their comments on my report card proof that I was, indeed, perfect, comments I was more than happy to translate into Spanglish for Mami and Papi.

"Yvonne is very smart. *¡Dice que yo soy* super smart!"

"Yvonne is an excellent student. *¡Dice que yo soy una* good student!"

"Yvonne is good at everything. *¡Dice que yo soy* good at *todo!*"

"Yvonne has the best handwriting. Dice que yo soy . . . uh, *¿cómo se dice* handwriting *en español?*"

"You must be so proud to have a daughter like Yvonne. *¡Dice que* you should be super proud *de tener una hija como yo!*"

Mami and Papi were indeed proud of me, Mami's joy expressed in the little gifts she gave me each time I got straight A's; new lip gloss or earrings from Avon, a new lunchbox or book bag, a brand-new Trapper Keeper, gifts I appreciated very much but no more than the happiness I saw on her face as she framed my report card or bragged about me to her family in Mexico.

"Yvonne is very smart," she would say on the phone. "*¡Y toca el piano!* You should hear her play, she's so talented."

No surprise, I developed an unhealthy obsession with school; a potential absence made me cry and beg for mercy. "I don't want to stay home, Mami, pleeeeease let me go to school! I don't even feel sick!" A fever of one hundred two meant nothing because I worried more about disappointing my teacher, hated that my perfect attendance record might be tainted by stupid bronchitis.

Placing her hand on my forehead to check for fever, I'd see the concern in Mami's eyes. "*Ay Dios mío*," she would say, "you are very sick." *Nervios* in full force, she would wring her hands as she left my bedroom, off to grab the family stash of Vick's VapoRub, the Latino cure for everything from the flu to a broken arm. When Vick's alone was not enough, she'd resort to the one thing sure to make me feel better: food. She cured my maladies with Vick's and Pizza Hut or Tylenol and McDonald's.

Yet in spite of my efforts in school and with piano, Mami's anxiety couldn't be tamed twenty-four seven because as kids, Raz and I fought and argued over almost everything, Mami's *nervios* spiraling out of control as she chased us around the house holding one of her *chancletas*, yelling at us for driving her crazy. We'd be sent to our rooms as punishment, our twenty-minute isolation ending as soon as Mami calmed down, a bowl of ice cream or a *paleta* her way of apologizing for her emotions.

Food was a constant throughout my childhood, my weapon of choice for every fear or concern, the endless snacks and treats adding several layers of fat to my body, a reality that didn't faze me because being a perfect student and pianist was all that mattered to me.

But then puberty.

The unexpected changes in my body made me sick to my stomach, what with rapidly growing breasts and nipples that darkened overnight, hair growing in all kinds of places, and widening hips. I became altogether too aware of my unmanageable, frizzy hair and bucked teeth—all of it coming together to make me look like a chubby rabbit with an out-of-control afro.

Being out in public was torture, what with all the grown men ogling me *that way* and making me feel ashamed of my budding breasts and widening hips, their eyes lingering on my chest and traveling down to my hips, my face turning beet red from the embarrassment.

I told Mami the attention made me uncomfortable, expecting her to sympathize and solve this horrible problem. "No, *mija*, there's nothing to be ashamed of," she said. "It would be worse if men didn't pay attention to you at all."

Funny how just a few words can screw you up for the rest of your life.

I started wearing baggy clothes to cover my body, which drove Mami crazy. "It's ninety-two degrees outside, *mija*, take off that ugly sweater!" I refused to take it off because my ugly green sweatshirt was a safety blanket, along with the XL Ocean Pacific T-shirts I slipped over my one-piece bathing suit at the pool or the beach. Not being fully aware of what was happening to my body scared me; covering my body made me hopeful that nobody would see the changes.

But one half of my family is Cuban, a tribe in which not a damn thing ever goes unnoticed.

Family members openly made comments about my *desarrollo*, i.e. puberty. They discussed my journey into womanhood whenever possible, conversations that made me want to crawl into a cave because nobody had prepared me for this journey to hell. My sex education had been a short film in school about the "birds and the bees" and a vague explanation from Mami, who couldn't look me in the eyes as she talked about my transformation into a woman. Sex was a taboo subject for Mami, and her version of sex education was delivered in clues I had to decipher with my very limited imagination.

"*Mija*, don't let a boy kiss you with his tongue. *Qué asco*."

"*Mija*, don't sleep with *un muchacho* until you are married, okay?"

"Keep your legs together, *mija*, and don't let him touch you down there."

These cryptic messages both confused and shamed me, gave me the impression that my body was something to hide, my sexual urges a cardinal sin, my desire to touch myself *down there* an absolute crime. I wanted to ask Mami questions, wanted to understand why her face turned bright pink whenever the subject came up, but she'd quickly change the subject and instead encourage me to go play the piano or read a book. I gathered that a change was coming, some kind of metamorphosis, but that's where my knowledge ended.

Mami got a sign in one of her dreams that my "change" would happen the summer between sixth and seventh grade, the tone in her voice making it seem like the second coming of Christ. She held fast to the notion that my baby fat would disappear and that every aspect of my life would change, causing me to jump out of bed every morning, my eyes hoping to see beautiful straight hair or teeth that fit in my mouth, breasts back to their normal size, and armpits devoid of yucky hair.

As she predicted, I found drops of blood on my panties a few days after the school year ended, and I thought, *Oh my God, I'm dying*, Mami's inability to be straightforward and that stupid video having failed to let me in on the big secret, namely that I would bleed heavily out of my vagina for six days straight, and that this monthly phenomenon would include crippling abdominal pain, irritability, bloating, uncontrollable emotions, and cravings.

Overnight the creepy looks intensified, what with every disgusting, hairy older man within a fifty-mile radius seeming to gravitate toward me. I wanted to scream whenever I caught someone staring at me, wanted to forget about being a respectful *señorita* and slap the creepy old guy with a hairy chest ogling me in the bakery section of Sedanos Supermarket, my frustration reaching a boiling point to see the smirk on his face.

I couldn't talk to any of my friends from school, because many of them were super excited about the changes in their bodies. Neither could I open up to Mami and share with her my horror and frustration, my period having become a joyous event she shared with the entire family even though I begged her to keep it a secret. No sooner had I gotten my period did she pick up the phone and call Tia Leya, who then proceeded to call every single person we knew and possibly some we didn't, just for the hell of it. "Did you hear? Yvonne has become a *señorita*." Whenever someone commented on my new status as a young woman, I'd pray for a hole in the ground to swallow me. At night, I'd pray to Jesus to turn back time and then cry myself to sleep, overwhelmed with confusion, anger, and shame because all of it felt weird and scary, like things were happening that I couldn't control.

But then *food.*

Heavy snacking carried me through that summer of hell and whereas Mami thought my baby fat would disappear, it developed into back fat that defeated my training bras and underwear, which she happily replaced with large panties to accommodate mammoth-sized maxi pads because tampons would clearly destroy my sacred virginity. Gaining weight didn't faze me; I was distracted by pain and rapidly changing moods, by maxi pads that made me walk like I'd ridden a horse for ten hours. Yet in spite of this misery, I looked forward to starting my seventh-grade year at Riviera Junior High School because school had long been my safe place, where teachers loved me for delivering the very best of my brain.

Several weeks before school started, I came down with a flu that confined me to bed and killed my appetite for nearly two weeks, resulting in significant weight loss I didn't notice until Mami took me shopping at J. Byron's Department Store for new clothes. School shopping days were like holidays for me, as afterward we would go to Lila's Restaurant for a *medianoche* sandwich. Mami was taken aback when I came out of the dressing room the first time, smiling broadly as she said, "Wow, *mija*, you look so different. ¡*Qué bonita!*"

Mami wasn't one to comment on my physical body, her words consequently making a huge impact on me as I went back into the dressing room and looked at my body from different angles, my eyes taking in the changes in my hips and belly. *Mami was right*, I thought, *my baby chub disappeared after all.* It pleased me that Mami was happy about something I didn't really do on purpose, and for the first time that miserable summer, I felt a little bit better about getting my period.

Mami's praise made me happy, but the attention I got on the first day of school took this happiness to a whole new level, which added to the excitement of going to a brand-new school and having my very own big girl locker. As I navigated the new hallways in search of each class-room, kids I'd known since the second grade stopped me to say hello, making me feel like a celebrity of sorts.

"Hey, Yvonne, you look really different. Like, better? I don't know. Who do you have for English?"

"Did you, like, lose weight or something? You look skinnier. Did you get your locker?"

"You've lost, like, a lot of fat or something. Who's your math teacher?"

I'd lost maybe ten pounds, but ten pounds in the seventh grade when kids notice everything is a big deal. Having never been praised for my appearance, the novelty of this attention excited me. Being a straight A student and pianist took a back seat to having a perfect body, all of my attention shifting to what I would wear, how I would look, whether or not anyone would make a comment.

Assuming I'd lost weight because of my period, I resumed my normal eating habits: a scoop of chocolate almond ice cream at night, two bowls of Cocoa Pebbles for breakfast. After a month, I stopped fitting into the nice new pants and blouses Mami had bought me, but I knew better than to ask for new clothes. Having grown accustomed to hitting the sales racks and watching Mami calculate just how much she could spend, I resorted to wearing my old clothes, my only consolation the knock off Sergio Valente jeans and Members Only jacket that I'd gotten for Christmas the year before. Being a "large" had never bothered me, but there was no place for a big girl like me in junior high, definitely no room for back fat or a big belly in the harsh new world of cliques and popularity in which I found myself.

I tried to tell myself it didn't matter, that I didn't need to be popular, but sitting in the cafeteria with the few friends I had from elementary school, I would catch myself staring at the cheerleaders and the boys who swarmed around them like bees to honey, frustrated that my thicker constitution had no chance of doing back flips or straddle jumps because I'd spent too much time hunched over eighty-eight ivory keys for the sake of mastering composers who cared nothing about popularity.

I began to compare myself to other girls, analyzed their every move in the hopes that I'd figure out the secret to a flat stomach and smooth legs. Like a sociopath in the making, I observed clusters of skinny and pretty American girls in the cafeteria as they giggled and passed notes, their lips shiny with cherry flavored lip gloss as they planned a slumber party, "Oh my God, I can't wait! We're going to have pizza and stay up all night!" They represented what I'd only read about in the many books I'd brought home from Westchester Public Library: an American life, complete with camping trips, a weekly allowance, and sleepaway summer camps—all of which fascinated me and made me wish that I'd been born into a different family, one that held family meetings to discuss conflicts or upcoming vacations, one that regularly listened to The Eagles instead of Celia Cruz or Tito Puente, one who resembled the family in *Happy Days* instead of *¿Qué Pasa, USA?*

In the privacy of my bedroom, with the cast of *The Outsiders* looking down on me from a poster on my wall, I'd grab the tire rolls around my midsection and squeeze them in frustration, wishing they'd deflate so I could get invited to a slumber party that Mami wouldn't let me attend anyway, her fear of someone sexually abusing me far too great to let me spend the night at some *fulanita's* house. Still, I dragged Mami into my fantasy world, begged her to take me to *el salón de belleza* so that my hair could be permanently straightened, an expensive endeavor that did nothing but ruin my already frizzy hair and leave it smelling much like a chemical plant.

The mirror in my bedroom became my enemy, what with its ability to highlight my imperfections: my overbite, my frizzy hair, and my hairy legs, which became a pressing concern after a boy in my Science class leaned over and whispered, "Your legs are soooo hairy. I think I see Tarzan!"

I asked Mami that same afternoon if I could shave them, and she swiftly replied, "No!"

A few days later, I tried again. "No!"

And again. "No!"

After the tenth time, Mami threw her hands up in the air and said, "Go ask your *papá*!" Off I went in search of the man who would decide the fate of my hairy-ass legs. I found him in the backyard, a cigarette dangling from his mouth as he watered the grass, our dog Spanky running back and forth with no real goal except to remind us that he was probably unstable.

"Papi, I need to ask you something."

"*Sí, mija*, what is it?"

I knew Papi had the final say, so I paused, worried he would say no. "Um . . . please please please can I shave my legs?"

He looked down, his eyes opening wide to see the amount of hair that blanketed my chubby legs. He pulled the cigarette out of his mouth and shrugged with indifference. "*Mija,* you can shave your *culo* for all I care. They're your legs!"

Yet even with smooth legs, I'd have a meltdown while getting dressed for school, the elastic on my pants digging into my waist sending me into a fit of emotion.

"You look fine, *mija,*" Mami would say.

"No, I don't!" I would cry. "*¡Estoy gorda!* I am so fat and ugly."

Raging hormones made it hard to control my emotions, and although food had always been my go-to, I was forced to accept that overeating was actually the problem. Each time I went for the bag of Doritos, the chubby little girl and the self-conscious seventh grader would go to battle, making it impossible to eat with abandon. Knowing nothing about nutrition, I questioned everything I ate. *Will potato chips make me gain weight? Will bananas make me super skinny?*

Given the nature of my birth and the urgent way in which I'd burst in to the world, diving headfirst into new friendships and venturing out of my comfort zone to engage in other activities would have been logical, but I did exactly the opposite the first two years of junior high school; being a talented pianist and a straight A student had not given me enough confidence to shake off the perpetual self-consciousness I wore like a heavy cloak as I walked from one classroom to the next, my books much like a shield to hide the hideous body in which I felt trapped.

Unable to concentrate on anything other than my looks, my grades slipped, a B and C on my report card sending me into a tailspin of emotions that I couldn't explain to Mami, who'd been observing my mood swings with empathy and understanding, none of the tears or fits of rage fazing her one bit because she chalked it up to *el desarrollo*, that stupid journey into womanhood.

Getting a B and C really bothered me, but it was no match for the mental and emotional bitch slap I felt to realize that talent and smarts weren't good enough anyway, those first few days of attention at the beginning of seventh grade having destroyed the bubble of innocence in which I'd been thriving.

I stood in front of my bedroom mirror at the end of eighth grade in nothing but underwear, Simple Minds blaring out of my boom box as I thought about how much I wanted to *forget about me*, a bold promise made to the world as I stared at the large, hideous body looking back at me. "I will be skinny, and I will be perfect." Sucking in my stomach, I repeated the words over and over. "I will be skinny, and I will be perfect." With nothing but common sense to guide me, I made a list of the changes I would make in my eating habits, having deduced that food was to blame for my chipmunk cheeks, the cellulite on my legs, my frizzy hair, sweaty armpits, and super heavy periods that debilitated me every single month.

1) No chocolate cake for breakfast
2) No pizza
3) No ice cream before bed
4) No Coke
5) No Doritos
6) No McDonald's after piano lesson
7) No donuts
8) No *pan Cubano* or *pastelitos*
9) No more *batidos*
10) No Nutter Butter cookies

Exercise was not on the forefront of my mind, my experiences in elementary school having been traumatizing and humiliating, the flexed-arm hang, one-mile run and sit-ups we had to do for the Presidential Fitness Test having inspired in me a sense of dread and fear rather than motivation to exercise. I'd grown up watching Mami hold her boobs in place as she jumped up and down and followed Jack LaLanne on TV, but she'd never remained dedicated to a regimen. Having spent much of their lives trying to consume calories rather than burn them, Mami's back rolls and Papi's belly were a clear sign of financial success, their version of the American Dream come true. Neither had they encouraged me to run and play outside, God forbid I break one of my precious piano fingers.

My PE teacher reminded us daily that regular exercise was important for health and for being thin, so I started doing jumping jacks, sit-ups, and leg lifts in the privacy of my bedroom, where nobody could see the rolls on my body jiggling all over the place. Adding music to my workouts made all of it more bearable, sweat pouring out of me as I moved around my small bedroom to Madonna's "Into the Groove" or stretched my legs to Wham's "Careless Whisper." Papi had bought me a ten-speed bike for my birthday, which I rode around our neighborhood every single day that hot summer, trying hard to keep gnats out of my mouth as I chanted over and over: "I will be skinny, and I will be perfect. I will be skinny, and I will be perfect."

BULL'S-EYE ON MY BACK

I WAS BORN ON AMERICAN SOIL, AND I AM PROUD TO HAVE been raised in a country with ample opportunities to succeed as well as with the freedom to express my views, but the blood that flows through my veins runs deep into the heart of *Latinoamérica*, my ethnicity equal parts *Cubana* and *Mejicana*, the *gringa* part of me unable to claim my identity because my very essence transcended my place of birth long ago.

Shaped by more than just our foods and music, my identity as a Latina is rooted in the core values we share as a people, in our ability to overcome hardships with tenacity, perseverance, and determination, in the underlying passion and respect for life that I've encountered in all of the Dominicans, Cubans, Guatemalans, Puerto Ricans, Colombians, Salvadorans, Chileans, Venezuelans, Nicaraguans, Hondurans, Bolivians, Peruvians, Ecuadorians, Costa Ricans, Argentines, and Mexicans who have crossed my path, our cultural differences not strong enough to drive us apart because combined we wrote the book on how to laugh, how to love, and how to *vivir*.

So yeah, I'm one proud Latina.

Half of me belongs to a lively Cuban family that prefers to shout instead of speak, the volume of our conversations a God-given right that nobody should dare question, *¿me oíste?* We use our hands, arms, and sometimes our whole body to get our point across. We love to kiss and hug and touch because we are a warm, affectionate people. We will always offer you something to eat because we assume everyone is hungry no matter the time of day, and your life simply won't be complete until you've had a heaping plate of *lechón*, white rice, and black beans. *¡No tengas pena, chico!*

We like to greet people with a kiss on the cheek instead of shaking hands, no matter the situation. Perfect strangers are lumped into this tradition, even and especially the few white people who decided to stay in Miami after the *Cubanos* took over.

Cubans are a crafty people, resourceful and creative in the most impressive of ways, those makeshift rafts and floating contraptions on which so many have left Cuba proof alone that Cubans *figure it out*. There's no need to worry about not having health insurance because there's always a family member who knows some guy who lives next door to *un tipo* who works with someone who can get you antibiotics for twenty bucks' cash. That same guy will hook you up to another guy whose girlfriend's father is good friends with *fulano de tal* who can fix the air-conditioner, or pull a tooth, or get a good deal on a cable box—a wonderful chain of I-know-a guy-who-knows-another guy-who-knows-this-guy-who-can-hook-you-up-for-nothing, *bro*.

The Mexican half of me belongs to a culture that keeps God and His team on speed dial, my relatives invoking either Jesus Christ or *la Virgin de la Guadalupe* for economic hardship, a global pandemic, a wayward child, an uncle with a drinking problem, a family conflict, and sometimes even for bingo, Mami muttering under her breath as she heads out the door, "*Ay Virgen Santa*, bless me with luck tonight so that I can win the jackpot." We add chile and *limón* to everything, be it sliced mango or ice cream or fried eggs, our love for jalapeños and all things spicy the possible reason we are so passionate and alive. We sing "Las Mañanitas" instead of the "Happy Birthday" song, and we'll go above and beyond to make you feel welcome at our *quinceañera* party because we are simply wired to love.

Combined, these two cultures have more things in common than they have differences, the approach to parenting one of those similarities and thank God because whether I am twenty-four, thirty-five, or fifty years old, I can move back home, no questions asked, my parents quick to remind me that it is still my home, "*Mija, esta es tu casa,*" Mami's refusal to take down my awful First Communion picture a testament to my existence. When I visit for a few days, Mami washes and folds my clothes, always offering to pack my suitcase or iron my outfit *para el avión*, because God forbid I get on a plane with wrinkled pants. For years I have been financially stable, but Mami won't let me leave without something to bring home, *por si las moscas*: two mangos, a new lipstick from Avon, a Tupperware full of *frijoles fritos*, three rolls of toilet paper.

I am impossibly vain, Mami having taught me to always put myself together, to brush my hair and fix my face before leaving the house, because what if I run into an acquaintance at the post office? "*Ay, Dios mío*, what will they think if you are a mess?" My taste in clothing and make-up has always been conservative, but it never stops me from admiring the many beautiful women across all ages who embrace their curves rather than hide them, and I envy their devil-may-care attitude as they strut around in super tight jeans and cute blouses that show off their ample cleavage, their sassy body language forever screaming, *¿Y qué?*

Our music is wonderfully diverse, with beats and sounds that trigger an involuntary response in my body, my hips swaying from side to side the second I hear salsa or merengue or bachata or reggaeton; mariachi music bringing a tear to my eye, my heart overwhelmed with emotion as the trumpets, vihuelas, and violins combined produce music that speaks to me, the passion with which they play a reminder that I descend from a long line of *chingones*.

I appreciate the differences and the similarities in both cultures, and I recognize that my upbringing was a blessed one, but I would be remiss to exclude the not-so-amazing cultural norms that quite frankly devastated my self-esteem.

My parents said and did nothing about my larger than average body. All throughout my childhood, they encouraged me to believe that I was beautiful and special, their unconditional love for me a solid foundation on which I could develop healthy core beliefs about myself and the world.

But.

Cubans take pride in their food and music and cigars and most of all, in their straight-up-in-your-face-not-going-to-lie manner of speaking, their mouths created solely for the purpose of giving you their thoughts and opinions, my relatives often failing to understand that their words were not always welcome. Their never-ending *críticas* poked holes in my foundation, my period having marked the beginning of a phase during which all my healthy core beliefs would be shot to hell.

We spent most holidays, birthdays, and special occasions with my Cuban tribe once we moved to Miami: aunts, uncles, cousins, and pretty much anyone who'd come to the US from *Güira De Melena, Cuba.* This large group of people freely commented on my appearance despite my efforts to make myself invisible, the endless stream of unsolicited opinions shared *for my own good,* of course.

"*Oye* (kiss), you are getting way too fat."

"Yvonnecita (kiss), *estás muy gorda.*"

"*Dame un besito* (kiss). *Pero* what's wrong with your hair? It smells funny."

"*Hola* (kiss), *mira que* you've gained so much weight."

"*Muchacha* (kiss), those pants are too small for you."

"*Niña, ven acá* (kiss), you need to stop eating *pastelitos.*"

Hyper-sensitive and vulnerable after I got my period, whatever love and patience I'd had for my relatives vanished overnight. I dreaded our Sunday visits to see my grandmother and aunt, loathed birthday parties, hated family gatherings, and especially despised baby showers where everyone reminded me that as a *señorita,* my sole purpose in life was to get married and *give* my husband a child, as though squeezing a human out of my vagina was the only way to establish my worth as a woman. On one occasion, an older woman decided to share her own experience with childbirth. I tried hard to stay focused on her bleached blond hair and bright red lipstick as she mapped out the ordeal from start to finish, her dedication to detail creating a visual that I will never in my life be able to unsee. "I didn't feel anything when they sliced open my vagina," her words creating in me a fear so profound that it paralyzed me in my seat.

Never did I attend a gathering of relatives and walk away unscathed. Their endless *críticas* of my appearance crushed me, but I couldn't retaliate because Mami raised me to be respectful, which translated into "You must be passive, submissive, and otherwise invisible." Humiliated and angry, I would find a place to sit where nobody could make comments about my weight or my hair, tears running down my face as I ate ham *croquetas* and wondered why everyone stopped asking me about piano or school, why their only focus seemed to be my physical appearance rather than my talent or brain, their words fueling the intense anger that drove me to make a bold promise at the end of eighth grade.

I will be skinny. I will be perfect.

Anger fueled my willpower and motivation, and it kept me strong whenever I wanted to eat a piece of Entenmann's chocolate cake, but my venture into proper dieting was not without its challenges.

My parents took pride in our overstocked fridge and pantry, in knowing that we were ready for a famine at all times. Even though Mami cooked traditional Mexican or Cuban dishes like *bistec empanizado or pollo con mole* for dinner, they stocked the fridge with chicken pot pies, frozen TV dinners, deli ham and cheese slices, Wonder bread, Doritos, Cocoa Pebbles, and every flavor of Chek soda. Mami often made comments about how blessed we were to have so much food, quick to remind us that she'd nearly starved to death as a child, words that plagued me with guilt and kept me from asking her to make changes. I decided to eat less and eliminate the foods I assumed were fattening, which was near everything.

Mami had always been supportive, her love for me so strong that she thought nothing of driving me to piano lessons every week or of running to Eckerd Drugs at the last minute because "I forgot I need a poster for school."

She thought it her duty to drive me to the library or to the movies, "Mami, can we see *Karate Kid* one more time pleeeease?" When we received a flyer in the mail advertising open registration for a bowling league at Bird Bowl, Mami had agreed to take me, it being the only thing besides piano that had interested me in the sixth grade. She had driven me every Saturday morning for a year and watched with excitement as I rolled a heavy orange ball toward ten pins at the end of a lane, Mami unable to contain her happiness whenever I got a strike, "*¡Así, mija, muy bueno!*"

But when it came to restricting calories and going hungry for the sake of being skinny, I completely lost her. I'd been wolfing down *pastelitos* and Farm Store donuts for all of my life, and my decision to eat less confused her.

"Mami, no, not so much. *Un poquito.* Less rice, less steak," I'd say at dinner as she piled food on our plates. I'd avoid eye contact because I knew she'd be worried.

"*¿Qué te pasa?* You don't feel good? Are you sick?"

"I'm okay, Mami, but I'm trying to lose weight."

"Lose weight? *¿Para qué?* You are *perfecta.*"

Papi would chime in. "*Mija*, you are beautiful. You don't need to lose weight."

After my piano lesson, Mami would offer to buy me a treat as usual. "Are you sure you don't want something from McDonald's?"

"*Sí*, Mami, let's just go home. I don't want McDonald's," I'd say, my mouth watering at the thought of a Big Mac with French fries.

"What about Burger King?"

"No, Mami, no Burger King."

"*Bueno*, *mija*," she'd say, her eyes a little sad. "*De todos modos*, I'm making enchiladas for dinner."

Knowing how much I loved Mami's cooking, I would mentally prepare myself by looking in the mirror, my hands grabbing the fat around my midsection and turning sideways so I could see the rolls of back fat that made me look like a linebacker, the frustration of not being skinny motivating me to ride my ten-speed bike around the block a few times before dinner. I'd join my parents for a walk around the neighborhood after dinner and remind myself to ignore the pound cake when I got home.

I will be skinny. I will be perfect. I will be skinny. I will be perfect.

My new diet and exercise routine kept my *nervios* under control; my new sense of calm helped me get through a few hours of piano practice without eating half a bag of Oreo cookies. Sunflower seeds replaced Doritos while I lost myself in whatever Nancy Drew book I was reading, the donuts I once enjoyed at bedtime and the loaf of toasted Cuban bread I shared with Raz on Saturday mornings banished from my life, little changes that, when combined, deflated the tire rolls around my midsection and allowed my cheekbones to make an appearance, my new look enhanced by the rapid growth spurt that brought me to five foot five inches.

Mami took me shopping for new clothes at the end of the summer. As I slid into new pants and blouses in the dressing room, I wondered if Mami would notice the changes again and say something. Her face lit up when I walked out of the dressing room, her eyes the size of quarters as she looked me up and down. "*Ay Dios mío*, you look so different. You have lost so much weight, *mija*. Wow." Pleased that she'd noticed, I walked back into the dressing room with a smile on my face, convinced that losing weight had been a great idea, as clearly it made other people happy.

I am skinny. I am perfect.

I walked out of the dressing room just in time to see Mami pull a blouse off a rack and admire it for a few seconds.

"That's pretty," I said. "Are you going to try it on?"

I asked even though I already knew the answer. The idea of Mami doing anything for herself was a far-fetched concept. Never did I see Mami go out with friends or engage in any kind of self-care like a manicure or weekly trips to *el salón de belleza,* her once a year hair appointment a sacred occasion during which she nervously checked the time, consumed with guilt for having chosen to spend a few hours focusing on herself instead of her family.

She hesitated, as though conflicted, and promptly returned the pretty blouse to the rack. "No," she laughed, as though dismissing a silly idea. "For what? I don't need new clothes. *A ver*, are you ready to go?"

My aunt and grandmother came over the day before I entered ninth grade, their loud voices sending me into a panic as I finished my hundred sit-ups to Journey's "Don't Stop Believing." I wanted badly to stay in my room, but I knew Mami would knock on my door and force me to *saludar.*

With my stomach in knots, I walked into the living room in sweatpants and a T-shirt, rivers of sweat running down my face and arms as I braced myself for the *críticas* I knew would come.

My aunt: "Yvonne (kiss). *Óyeme, pero* what are you doing that you look so skinny?" She looked to my mother. "Is she sick?"

My grandmother: (kiss) "*¡Qué flaca*! Be careful, don't get too skinny, eh?"

I took their screwed-up votes of confidence and went back to my room, a triumphant smile on my face.

I am skinny. I am perfect.

THE ELEPHANT ON MY CHEST

WANTING TO LOOK PERFECT ON THE FIRST DAY OF NINTH grade, I spent hours the night before trying on different outfits, settling on a pair of knock off Guess jeans that pronounced my flat tummy and thinner hips and a blouse with wide sleeves to show off my skinny arms. Mami had taken me to get a much-needed haircut, my brave new hairstyle cemented with AquaNet hairspray as I walked into first period, one year older but still remarkably self-conscious. I took a seat in the front row, purposefully avoiding eye contact, my weight loss and new hair not enough to calm my nerves as we waited for the teacher to call attendance.

Mrs. Sabarots had been my French I teacher, a class in which I'd gotten a nasty, shameful C. In a cheerful voice that reminded me of a parakeet, she acknowledged each student as she called their name, taking a moment to ask about their summer before she moved on down the list in her black attendance book.

"Here!" I said, when she called my name. Mrs. Sabarots looked up from the attendance book, her eyes growing wide as she took off her reading glasses.

"*Mon Dieu,* is that really you, Yvonne?"

I nodded, thirty pairs of eyes boring into me making the hair on the back of my neck stand.

Mrs. Sabarots smiled. "Looks like you had a great summer, Yvonne. You look amazing, *so thin.*" She winked. "*Trés bon!*"

I smiled broadly, her compliment having opened a door in my brain through which happiness now flowed into every crevice of my body, her words reverberating in my gullible mind. *You look amazing, so thin. You look amazing, so thin. You look amazing, so thin.* For the rest of the day, I paid little attention in my classes and instead focused on the three-minute break we had between classes, excitement coursing through me as I walked the hallways and received more compliments from my peers.

I was drunk on praise and attention when I walked into the school cafeteria during lunchtime. A popular cheerleader ran up to me, a huge smile on her face. "Yvonne! Oh my God, you look *so* skinny and *so* good! What did you do? I need to lose a few pounds. You should try out for the JV cheerleading squad at Southwest High! Tryouts are at the end of the year. You'd love it! Anyway, I gotta go, bye!" She left as quickly as she arrived, her beautiful blond hair, perfect body, and pimple-free skin causing every head to turn in admiration. Excited about the possibility of being a cheerleader, I threw away my lunch, too afraid it would cause my body to balloon overnight and thus ruin everything.

This loose invitation to be a super cool, super popular, super awesome cheerleader was all the encouragement I needed to become fully obsessed with my physical appearance and weight loss. Rather than continue on what I thought was a "normal" diet, I began to trim my meals, at times skipping both breakfast and lunch and sticking to a very small portion for dinner. Each morning I'd stand before the mirror and check my body for changes, hopeful that I had lost more weight, at times worried that I might not be skinny or pretty enough to try out for the cheerleading squad at the end of the school year. It made me nervous that people at school had stopped commenting on my weight, had stopping saying, "Yvonne, like, you've gotten *so so* skinny," so I relied on my hyper-critical family members to provide me with a reality check, one they happily forked over each and every time I saw them.

"Yvonne," my aunt would say, "you look sick. You really need to eat more. *Estás demasiado flaca.*"

"You are way too skinny," my grandmother would say. "Cuban men like some meat on their women." *Ew, super gross.* "You'll never find a *novio* if you're all skin and bones."

Skin and bones worked just fine for me, because the last thing I wanted was any kind of attention from hairy, nasty, disgusting older Cuban men who liked to scan my body from head to toe, their beady, hungry eyes pausing on my breasts before their slow descent to my hips and thighs. If "skin and bones" meant I'd never again have to deal with that bullshit, I was willing to starve myself for the rest of my whole life, but still I craved attention from boys my age. Rather than make me recoil in disgust, the admiration I got from boys at school made me feel special, but it also made me shy and awkward, because I didn't know the rules of dating.

My first lessons on the "rules" were delivered to me by Papi, whose approach to just about everything in my life was completely hands off. I was standing in our kitchen, debating whether or not I should call a boy from school, a nice guy with big brown eyes who'd asked me for my phone number after Math class. I'd scribbled it on a piece of paper, my hands shaking and my ability to speak stuck somewhere between my brain and my vocal chords, and he'd slipped his phone number into my hand. "Okay, uhm, thanks," I'd said, before I walked away, convinced the heat on my face would probably set another student on fire.

Papi walked into the kitchen just as I was conferring with Mami, who'd surprised me when she said I could have *un amiguito* so long as I kept my legs closed and my tongue inside my mouth.

"Mami, *¿qué piensas?* Should I call him?"

Papi poured himself a shot of *cafecito*, his left hand rubbing his "I might be having twins" belly.

"*Bueno, mija*," she said, "did he say he was going to call you?" She was focused on her *carne con papas* and seemed a little distracted.

"He did. I think. But maybe he lost my phone number. Or maybe he's waiting for *me* to call."

Mami tilted her head to the side. "Maybe."

Papi kept quiet until the moment I picked up the yellow phone attached to the wall, the cord attached to the handset long enough to strangle ten people. He grabbed the phone right out of my hand and hung it up. "*No, señora.*"

"I can't talk to a boy? Mami said it was okay."

He laughed. "Oh, you can talk to a boy all you want, *pero* don't you dare call him. *Ni te atreves.*"

"*Pero* why not?"

"*Mija*, let me tell you something. If *un muchacho* really wants to talk to you, there's nothing on earth that will stop him from calling you, *¿me oíste?* And if he doesn't call you, *mira*, forget about him. He's not worth your time."

"So I can't call him? Never ever?"

"*Claro que* you can call him, *pero* for now, wait. Let's see if he's really interested in you." He winked, a loud fart marking his departure as he walked out of the kitchen. Mami rolled her eyes and covered her mouth and nose with a kitchen cloth, the smell bad enough to make me forget about calling anyone.

A few days later, I was still thinking about whether or not to call my brown-eyed suitor when Papi pulled into a gas station on our way to the Winn-Dixie for groceries. Papi handed me the cash, and I went inside to pay while he got ready to pump the gas. The young man working the register smiled at me, and I smiled back as my eyes landed on the box of Blow Pops next to the register.

"Do you want one?" he asked.

"Yeah, *pero* I don't have any more money. Let me go ask—"

"No, it's okay. *Mira,* take it." He handed me a cherry Blow Pop and winked. "It's on me."

I took the Blow Pop and thanked him. Getting something for free was totally cool, so I told Papi, whose eyebrows joined together in some kind of reaction I couldn't read, but which I sensed was *no bueno.*

He pulled his wallet out of his pocket. "Here," he said, handing me a dollar, "go inside and pay for it, and then buy a few more with the change."

"Oh. But. He said it was free, that I could have it. We don't have to pay for it, Papi."

"*No, señora,*" he said, shaking his head. "Let me tell you something. Nothing is free. *Anda*, go pay for it."

Aside from random "Let me tell you something" moments, Papi was so laid back he may as well have been horizontal, his decision to let me go on dates *sin chaperona* a complete surprise to everyone given the reputation of Cuban fathers. My first car date with an older boy a few months later was pre-empted by a lecture, "*Mija*, I'm letting you go on this date *porque* I trust you, eh? *Así que* don't do anything to ruin that trust." His words were so impactful that indeed I didn't do anything except kiss and rub and grind and touch, whatever urges I had to go *all the way* repressed by the knowledge that Papi trusted me a great deal, believed me to know how to make the right choices. Having always been the good daughter, I kept my legs closed and that sacred part of me intact, every other part of my body fully explored and lips swollen from hours of kissing, my hair in disarray as I'd walk in the door praying that Mami wouldn't notice anything. But Mami would be lost in *The Exorcist* or *Nightmare on Elm Street*, Freddy Krueger and Papi's faith in me possibly the mechanisms that stopped her from caring about what was going on *down there*.

Yet rather than focus on boys and relationships, I obsessed instead on getting down to skin and bones, which did little for the physical strength I would need as a cheerleader if I had to shoulder the weight of another human or throw someone up into the air. I ventured into team sports and joined the softball, basketball, and volleyball teams at school in the hopes that I might get into better shape than what I'd been able to achieve with Madonna and Wham! in the privacy of my bedroom.

Mami happily drove me to Tamiami Park, where I joined a league cheerleading team that didn't require tryouts, a small squad with which I was able to learn the basics of cheerleading and get somewhat closer to achieving a perfect split. Mami would find me in my room, sweat pouring down my face as I stretched my legs and hips beyond what was normal, a concerned look on her face as she shook her head from side to side. "Ay *mija*, I don't know, that looks bad for you, *válgame Dios. Ten mucho cuidado*, ¿*eh?* Stretching like that might cause you to lose your virginity." But I didn't give a damn about losing my virginity; I cared more about losing my chance to be a cheerleader.

I was much more involved in extracurricular activities than I'd been the first two years of junior high school, and my grades, which might have suffered, only improved, my obsession with weight loss a minor distraction as once again I earned straight As. Outside of new activities and interests, I became close friends with Daisy, a girl whose brother played baseball with Raz at Tamiami Park, her Cuban family so beyond amazing and respectable that Mami relented and let me spend the night almost every weekend, our stay up until 6:00 A.M. sleepovers a marathon of conversations about true love as we listened to everything from Lionel Richie to Heart. Daisy was one year older and everything I aspired to be: tough and sassy and bold and sexy in a way that most grown women couldn't pull off, this mature beyond her years girl not once making me feel weird or different. She was not at all self-conscious; getting super skinny or being popular was nowhere on her radar. She was unapologetically loud, funny, and outgoing, and rather than be ashamed of her curvaceous hips, thighs, and breasts, Daisy flaunted both. Her ability to be open and accepting of her own body disarmed me, and I relaxed around her, her authenticity a haven for my fear of not being pretty or skinny enough.

I had friends, a new body, a chance to be a popular cheerleader and even though it had only lasted a few months, I'd had my first "for real" boyfriend, my alarming disinterest in piano the only downside to my new reality. I no longer practiced as much, nor did I look forward to my weekly lessons with Martha. Ninth grade coincided with my last year of piano studies and consequently my final exam, my graduation dependent on how well I'd mastered certain pieces of music, challenging songs on which I had trouble focusing because images of me as a popular cheerleader had flooded my brain and shoved Beethoven's "Sonata Pathétique" and Ernesto Lecuona's "Malagueña" far from my mind.

Shortly before the end of ninth grade, my parents drove me to see Olga, an elegant Cuban woman who facilitated piano exams for the Fine Arts Conservatory in her beautiful Coral Gables home. We waited in the living room along with other examinees, my heart beating wildly and butterflies in my stomach as one by one, we were called into the examination room.

Olga called my name, her eyes scanning the living room as she no doubt expected to see the large version of me. "*Ay Dios mío,*" she said loudly as I walked toward her, the approval in her eyes making me blush. "*Vaya, pero* what a difference. You have lost so much weight, Yvonne, and you are beautiful! *¡Qué hermosa!*" She kissed me on the cheek and gave my skinny arm a quick squeeze.

Thrilled that she'd noticed my new look, I followed her into the exam room, a wide-open space with wooden beams stretching across the vaulted ceiling, large windows all around, and French doors that opened onto a patio with wrought iron furniture, a breathtaking view of a pristine golf course in the background.

A midnight black grand piano stood boldly in the middle of the room, its presence instantly putting me at ease because the piano had never cared for the size of my body; my eating habits and weight gain had been no concern for the eighty-eight ivory keys that offered themselves to me each and every time. Piano had always been a safe haven for me, the realization that I was walking away from it forming a lump in my throat.

Caught off guard by my feelings, I sat down at the piano and did a few scales to warm up, my heart breaking at the memory of Papi pulling the tiny toy piano off the shelf at Toys R Us, the tears in his eyes each time I played "Malagueña," his nostalgia for Cuba getting the best of him; the memory of Mami driving us through Coral Gables after piano lessons, the wide tunnel of huge Banyan trees along Coral Way providing shade as I ate my Happy Meal, Mami refusing to take some of my French fries because "No, *mija*, I'm not hungry."

Fighting back tears, I took a deep breath, pausing for a moment before I began to play my final pieces because I needed my brain to be devoid of thoughts and memories and visions so I could focus only on flawless execution. Up and down the keys my fingers moved, my ability to remember exactly which keys to press still a mystery as I lost myself in the music of my good friends Bach, Rachmaninoff, Beethoven, and Mozart; Chopin and Lecuona carrying me across the finish line two hours later, my fingers slowly coming off the keys one last time as I remained seated, exhaustion and relief hitting me all at once.

Olga stood up and walked over to the piano, her arms opened wide to embrace me as I stood up to face her. "Ay Yvonne, you are so talented, *¡mi niña!* May God always bless those hands of yours."

"Thank you, Olga."

She took a step back, her arms on mine. "Just look at you, all grown up, *toda una mujersita*. Now let me go get your parents, *¿sí?* I want to talk to them."

I sat on the couch in front of Olga's desk, a huge bowl of candy on the coffee table tempting me.

Olga walked back into the room with my parents in tow. "Take a seat. Make yourselves at home. *¿Quieren un cafecito?*"

Papi and Mami sat next to me on the couch. "*No, gracias.*"

After a few minutes of small talk, Olga cleared her throat. "*Bueno*, I called you in here because now that Yvonne is finished with her formal studies, I want to propose something." She winked at me as though we shared a secret. "I want *la niña* to continue her studies with me. *¿Qué te parece?* We need to develop her talent, get her ready for a different stage, because I think Yvonne can someday be a concert pianist." She looked at me again, smiling and nodding. "She has so much talent, *Señor Castañeda.*"

I felt sick to my stomach. *This cannot be happening,* I thought.

"*Ay Dios mío,*" Mami said as she looked at Papi.

"*Mira, Señora Olga,*" Papi said, "I love the idea, *pero la realidad es que* we don't have the money to pay you for lessons." Olga was an expensive piano teacher and charged forty dollars an hour, each lesson lasting two hours. Meeting Olga's eyes, Papi seemed not at all embarrassed by our limited finances, his pride in being able to provide for his family all he needed to stand tall.

Olga sat up straighter. "*Pero un momento,*" she said. "Who said you would have to pay me? You misunderstood me. I want to take her on as a *pro bono* student, so you wouldn't have to pay me anything."

Oh crap, I thought.

All three heads turned to look at me, their expectation

that I jump for joy ultimately shattered because I couldn't stop staring at the armrest of the sofa. I was too afraid to make eye contact with Mami's *nervios*, Papi's pride, and Olga's generosity, conflict tearing through me like an emotional tornado.

My new, thin body held the promise of a fun life: cheerleading and new friends and pep rallies and sports and hopefully another boyfriend—all of the things I'd read in books and seen in movies, a life I'd been dreaming about but had never thought possible, and in this new world there was no room for piano. I'd grown tired of being a pianist-on-demand for my parents whenever we had new guests at the house, these requests for a song or two or ten often sparking anger and frustration that I never knew how to handle because I couldn't be disrespectful to them. "*Mija*, can you play '*Malagueña*' for so and so?" Or "Yvonne, come out of your room, please, and play a few songs for *la visita*." Of course I'd play, a knot in my stomach as I worried about hitting a wrong note and therefore disappointing our hopeful guests.

I couldn't imagine more years of lessons and endless hours of practice, couldn't stomach more random requests for mini concerts, the fear of disappointing my parents very real, and the pressure to make a decision suddenly feeling like an elephant on my chest.

"*Entonces*, Yvonne, what do you think?" Olga asked me.

I looked up to meet Olga's hopeful stare. "No . . . *gracias*. I don't want to do that. I don't want to study piano anymore."

"*What!*" they all said in unison.

I kept my eyes focused on Olga, silently pleading with

her to understand my fourteen-year-old brain and its desire for something new. "I love playing the piano, but I want to try other things."

Olga cocked her head to one side. "Things like what?"

"I don't know, maybe a sport."

"*¿Un deporte?*"

"Uh-huh, yeah." I prayed she wouldn't ask more questions because I didn't want to explain pom poms and splits.

Olga looked positively crushed. "*Qué pena*, Yvonne. With that talent, you could get a music scholarship. Don't you want to go to college?"

I shrugged. "Maybe."

She sighed, defeated. "*Bueno*, if you change your mind, let me know, *pero* don't wait. This opportunity won't be around forever, okay? Becoming a concert pianist takes a lot of work and time." *Exactly.* As we walked out, she gently squeezed my arm. "Good luck, Yvonne."

Mami and Papi were silent on the way home, choosing to smoke instead of talk, the ashes landing on my face as they flicked their cigarettes out the window, but who was I to complain? My heart sank to the bottom of my flat stomach when Papi drove right past the Canton Dragon Chinese Restaurant, the realization that there would be no celebration dinner confirmation that I'd totally screwed up.

Plopped face down on my bed, conflict continued to tear through me. Knowing my parents were disappointed, I wished we'd talked about it on the way home, but we were not a Brady Bunch kind of family.

I heard a knock on my bedroom door and sat up. "Come in." Papi came into my bedroom and closed the door. *Oh no*, I thought, *here it comes.*

Papi was the master of painful lectures and discourses that always reduced Raz and me to tears, his soft voice and patient demeanor his way of letting us know we had disappointed him. Carefully choosing his words, Papi would talk about how hard he worked and how much he sacrificed for us, our pleas for him to spank us and get it over with falling on deaf ears because he would say, "Oh no, hitting you won't teach you anything." We'd sob uncontrollably and promise to never again fight over the last bowl of Cocoa Pebbles or the last jelly donut. I looked around my bedroom for a box of tissues as he sat down next to me.

"*Mija*, I want to talk to you."

I gulped. "Okay, Papi."

He paused, contemplating what to say. "*Mija,* I want to ask you for one favor, okay?" I nodded. "*Mira*, I will never tell you what to do with your life, eh? *Es tu vida*. You don't want to play piano no more? *Bueno, es* okay. *Pero* I want you to make for me one promise."

"Of course, Papi."

"*Mija*, I came to this country from Cuba, and I work so hard in construction *porque* I never have no good education. *Mira estas manos*." He showed me his calloused hands. "*Mija*, you have choices, *así que* promise me you will get education, you will go to college, and you won't get married until you have good job, career, your own *dinero*, okay? *Porque* if you get married and it doesn't work out, then what? You need to survive on your own, *resolver. ¿Está bien*? What do you think?"

I put my arms around him. "*Claro que sí*, Papi. I promise you." I sealed my promise with a kiss on his cheek.

"Ah, very good, very good," he said. "*Bueno*, let's go eat Chinese food because I'm starving. *¡Vámonos!*"

The four of us sat around a table at Canton Dragon Chinese Restaurant happily sharing two pupu platters and a large order of fried rice. I was relieved to be back in my parents' good graces, but I couldn't stop looking at Papi's hands, calloused and worn out from working construction, and Mami's eyes, which always held a hint of worry, of fear, as though hesitant to believe we lacked for nothing.

MEJICO LINDO

AT FOURTEEN YEARS OLD, I HAD NO REAL CONCEPT OF identity and no pressing need to categorize myself as either American or Cuban or Mexican or Latina or Hispanic. All I knew was that sometimes my Cuban family annoyed the shit out of me, and that the more they rattled my nerves, the less I wanted to connect with my Cuban roots, especially when I was forced to dance salsa or merengue with an uncle or a distant relative during a family party. That they expected me to move the hips with which I wasn't yet comfortable or shake the breasts that made me feel shame was simply unfair and rude. Dancing in front of the people who constantly judged and criticized me made me feel as though my flaws and imperfections were on display. I would feel the blood rushing to my face and sweat forming under my armpits, discomfort so unbearable that I would yank my hands away from whomever was holding me hostage and storm off in a huff, the fear of Mami yelling at me for being disrespectful not enough to stop me from walking away.

The more I felt shoved into all things Cuban, the more I rebelled and drifted more toward the interests of my white American counterparts. Rather than learn to dance salsa, I listened to Van Halen and Journey, fell in love with Rob Lowe and John Stamos, and although I couldn't identify with any of the cast members, I couldn't miss an episode of *The Facts of Life* or *Family Ties*.

Planning a *quinceañera* celebration was out of the question, as I couldn't picture myself enjoying a party during which I would wear something akin to a wedding dress and be celebrated for my official entry into womanhood. Hell no. The thought of my relatives making any reference to my "future" wedding filled me with dread and tied my stomach up in knots. Papi and Mami did not press the issue, and whether that was out of respect or due to financial constraints, I will never know or care. Only once did Mami broach the subject of posing for formal pictures, to which I replied by emphatically shaking my head, "No way, Mami. I don't want that. Save your money."

Neither was my Mexican identity something I thought about unless Mami pulled the giant *sombrero* off the wall and danced around it during a New Year's Eve party, an event usually preceded by a few shots of tequila or mezcal. These parties would often end with my Cuban relatives singing loudly to "El Rey" by Vicente Fernandez, the copious amount of tequila they had consumed having made them temporarily Mexican and therefore able to join Mami in her nostalgia for *Mejico lindo*.

Other than a few brief vacations in Tijuana and Ensenada when we had lived in California, I hadn't spent much time in Mexico. My memories of these vacations had more to do with the strong salty smell of the Pacific Ocean and less with culture and identity. Mami had taken me and Raz to visit her family in Guadalajara when I was eight years old, but my memories of that trip were vague. Once in a blue moon, Papi would drive us all the way down to Homestead for "real" Mexican food, since it was one of the cities in Florida with a large migrant population, but occasional trips to *"El Toro Taco"* and family parties during which Mami and Vicente Fernandez shared a moment were not enough for me to feel connected to my Mexican roots.

The only identity into which I felt comfortable slipping was that of a high school cheerleader. With piano out of the way, I devoted all of my free time to stretching my legs and practicing straddle jumps and making sure that I looked the part from head to toe. Being chosen for the squad was a huge deal because it would pretty much guarantee that I would be popular and cool, a status I wanted badly. Nothing else mattered to me, and when Mami announced that we'd be taking a trip to Mexico at the end of the summer, I gave it little thought, my breath temporarily suspended until I got the news that I'd officially been chosen.

So thrilled was I to be a cheerleader that I paid little attention to our impending trip until Mami put an empty suitcase on my bed and told me to start packing. Neither Raz nor I were excited about the trip, both of us having entered a stage in our lives during which we yearned to spread our wings and be free from family obligations and from what we perceived would be a boring vacation. Raz had discovered American girls, and he was busy falling in love with every blond-haired, blue-eyed goddess within a five- mile radius. Rather than chase *muchachos*, I wanted to wear my uniform all day and practice my routines, wanted time to fantasize about my brand-new awesome life, wanted to prepare for what I believed would be an epic high school experience. Going to Mexico felt all wrong, as though not staying focused on my new life might make all of it disappear. It made me nervous to disconnect from my dream come true, but choosing to stay home was simply not an option.

We boarded an Eastern Airlines flight on a Saturday in early August. *Nerviosa* and terrified of flying, Mami knocked over a cup of coffee midflight when the plane hit turbulence, the warm liquid spreading all over my white jeans as she muttered under her breath and asked Jesus to keep the plane from crashing, "*Ay Jesucristo, por favor* keep us safe and please help the pilot fly the plane."

Our first flight landed in Mexico City less than four hours later, the immigration officer's face serious as he stamped Mami's passport and checked mine and Raz's birth certificates. We headed toward the lounge to await our connecting flight, where Mami insisted on trying to remove the stain in my jeans by using a paper napkin that she wet with the tip of her tongue, as though saliva had become the new bleach.

It was in this departure lounge that I fell in love for the first time, not with a boy but with people watching, this being the first time in my young life that I found myself sitting in an international airport. My eyes followed the dark-skinned heavyset woman gripping the hand of a little girl with long black hair, her eyes tired and worried as she looked around for a place to sit. *She looks so scared,* I thought, *and what a cute little girl.* My gaze shifted to the beady-eyed man in a dark suit sitting across from us, his hands trembling slightly as he took a drag on a cigarette. *I wonder if he's nervous,* I thought. *Maybe he hates flying, too.* My eyes wandered and landed on a well-dressed older couple sitting at a table, their blank stares and silence making me wonder if they preferred to be in hell rather than together. *She looks so sad. I'm going to smile if she looks at me.* With curiosity, my eyes tracked the young man wearing a backpack the size of Texas, a map in his hands as he walked through the lounge on his way to somewhere. *Where is he from?* I wondered. *And where is he going?* Too soon our flight was announced over the loudspeaker. My eyes connected briefly with the older woman as I followed Mami and Raz, and in that brief moment of hesitation during which I contemplated what to do, she gave me a warm smile that lit up her entire face, an acknowledgment that made me feel as though we shared a secret.

Our connecting flight brought us to Guadalajara less than one hour later. Squinting my eyes, I tried to see through the pouring rain as the plane slowed to a halt, the smell of *tierra mojada* coming up to greet me as we stepped off the plane and down a flight of stairs to a small bus that would transport us to the terminal. We huddled close together on the bus, the cool air a welcome change from the awful humidity in Miami that always screwed up my hair.

As we waited for our bags, it occurred to me that I didn't really know anyone in Mami's family, the thought of meeting complete strangers suddenly making me nervous and ever more self-conscious. *Is my shirt wrinkled? Does my hair look okay? I should have brushed my teeth in the bathroom. I wish I didn't have this stain in my pants. Maybe I should've worn my other jeans.* As we picked up our bags, I wondered which of our relatives would be there to greet us. We walked into the arrivals lounge, my eyes scanning the area and immediately landing on a very large group of people waving their arms and yelling loudly. *"Hilda!! Hilda!!"* They rushed to greet us, my smile awkward and my palms sweating as an army of uncles and cousins and aunts surrounded us, all of them led by Abuela Meche, the matriarch of this enormous family, her smile warm and genuine as she hugged both me and Raz and kissed us several times on the cheek.

Mami made introductions. "This is your cousin Maribel, say hello. This is your cousin Susy, give her a kiss. This is your Tia Yoli, give her a hug. This is your Tio Miguel, shake his hand." Whereas my curiosity about perfect strangers had been strong at the airport, it only grew around my relatives, the questions that jumped into my brain at once eliminating whatever fears I'd had that I would feel awkward or self-conscious. My relatives came from a completely different world, yet I immediately felt a connection that took me by surprise. In their eyes, I saw my innocent curiosity reflected back at me, realized that they too wanted to know more about me and Raz, their *primos* from *El Otro Lado*. I let out a breath I hadn't realized I'd been holding, felt relief when nobody said, "You're too fat" or "You're too skinny" or "Your hair is a mess" or "There's a stain on your pants." We slipped comfortably into mindless chatter as we climbed into several VW bug taxis and made our way toward their home.

They lived near *el centro,* in a tiny apartment nestled within an old convent that had long ago been converted to living spaces. It was hard to imagine anyone doing any kind of living in those cramped quarters because crammed under one roof, we had nine cousins, two aunts, three uncles, and my badass grandmother, *Abuela Meche*, a beast of a woman who'd finished raising eighteen children only to find that her strength would be tested in the cruelest of ways when one of her daughters, my Tia Bertha, passed away at thirty-three years old. My aunt's sudden and tragic death had made orphans of eight children, ages three months to fourteen, and although consumed with grief and poor beyond comprehension, Abuela Meche had assumed responsibility for the eight orphans because *solo Dios sabe lo que hace.* Tio Ramón lived not inside the apartment but under a tarp on the roof, his commitment to fresh air and peace and quiet one that nobody questioned.

The other fourteen people shared three rooms: a larger room with three full-size beds, a room with a small sofa and dining room table, and a smaller room with two beds, one full sized and one twin. They made space for us by giving Raz, Mami, and me the full-size bed in the small bedroom next to Tio Javier, who slept on the twin bed and snored so loud that the room shook, our initial frustration eventually turning into laughter because Tio Javier would often fart in his sleep and wake himself up.

Abuela Meche cooked meals on a gas stove tucked into an alcove; she made *frijoles a la olla,* warmed up tortillas, and scrambled fresh eggs from *el mercado.* Tia Yoli sometimes used the burner flame to light up a cigarette when she couldn't find matches, which always made me worry her long eyelashes would catch fire and scorch the rest of her beautiful face. We pulled a curtain to give us privacy when we used the toilet located in a narrow closet space, and we pulled up fresh water from a well in the patio area and boiled it on the stove to take a bath, an old plastic container the only way to pour water all over our bodies as we stood shivering and naked in a kiddie pool, Mami shielding us with a towel for privacy.

Our bright American clothes and nice shoes garnered plenty of stares everywhere we went. Women young and old openly gawked at Raz as we walked around *Mercado San Juan De Dios* or *Plaza Tapatia.* As I walked to the *tiendita* on the corner with one of my cousins to get Mami a pack of cigarettes, the attention from strangers would make me blush from head to toe, my skinny body having failed to guarantee impenetrable confidence and self-esteem.

My cousin Lorena would giggle at the attention. "*Tia*," she would say to Mami, "*mi prima* Yvonne is so pretty. Everyone stares at her."

This new experience with my Mexican family was so refreshingly different and fun that after a few days, I found myself singing along to Hombres G and Juan Gabriel as we squeezed in around the dining room table to play *lotería* with pinto beans as place markers. I slipped easily into a Mexican dialect of Spanish as I sat on the front doorstep with my cousin Maribel, who patiently answered all of my questions about her boyfriend and school and life.

Something deep within me sprang to life when we walked past *Plaza de los Mariachis*, the combination of trumpets and violins filling me with a sense of home, of belonging, of love for a country about which I still knew very little. Mami bought us hot ears of grilled corn smothered in butter and topped with cotija cheese from a street vendor, a delicious treat that we devoured as we listened to the *músicos* belt their sorrowful tunes of love and betrayal, of *desgraciados* and *traicioneras*.

Mami had asked me and Raz to pack a suitcase with all the clothes we no longer wore or wanted, the gesture lost on me until I saw my cousin Lorena trying on one of my old blouses, the happiness on her face to have something new to wear causing a lump to form in my throat as the harsh reality of their situation smacked me in the face. We were not wealthy ourselves, but our American *dólares* went much further in Mexico, allowing Mami to pay for everyone as we huddled around a street side taco stand eating *tacos de barbacoa* or piled into a *paletería* for popsicles.

They cherished food in a way that was foreign to me; they never complained or questioned what was offered. Mami had reminded us often that we were fortunate to have so much, but I don't know that I'd truly understood what she meant because Raz and I had never known anything different; we'd always had a bountiful pantry and fridge with options galore, this blessed life one that I took for granted until I saw the excitement in Karina's eyes as I handed her a *paleta de mango*, her three years on earth having been marked by death and loss rather than the freedom to be a child. Karina had taken the paleta from my hand, her eyes sparkling with joy. "*¿Y el chile?* Can I have chile for my *paleta?*"

That they appreciated every single bite of their tacos or *birria* made my own obsession with weight loss and diet seem trivial and stupid and grossly out of place, causing me to feel shame for being worried about the number of calories in a bowl of *pozole*. They didn't seem at all preoccupied with their own bodies or with trying to be skinny, and unlike many of my Cuban relatives, they refrained from making comments about my appearance. Rather than fixate on my physical body, they were curious to know me as a person, not as an object to be criticized and judged, and in this space, I felt temporarily liberated from my own obsession.

There was no mention of my Aunt Bertha's death, for in this three-bedroom apartment in *Sector Libertad*, there was simply no room for the grief and pain of their unimaginable loss. On the occasion that Mami broached the subject with Abuela Meche, my grandmother quickly shut her down, her voice stern as she reminded her that we must move forward, whatever emotions Mami might have wanted to process dismissed with a few choice words that I heard often: "*Hay que seguir adelante, Hilda. Ni modo.*"

Abuela Meche was not immune to emotion, however. With so many people in her care, she lost her temper often and yelled, the large number of children she'd raised causing her to forget their names, which only made everyone laugh. "¡Lore! ¡Claudia! ¡Gabriela! ¡Susy! *Válgame Dios*, I must be losing my mind. ¡Yoliiiiii! *¡Por el amor de Dios*, I told you to turn off the iron!" Abuela Meche's anger was explosive, intense, and scary, my little cousins Mario and Carlitos taking the brunt of it each time they got into a squabble, which was daily. Mami would intervene and try to help, even though Papi explicitly told her not to get involved. "Their problems are none of your business," he'd said at the airport.

I had so much for which to be grateful: running water, food, and clothing, as well as things I didn't really need but without which I felt I couldn't live: my own television, my own boom box, my own bedroom. But none of these things had ever brought me the kind of unconditional happiness I felt around my family in Mexico. The love I felt for them took me by surprise, a profound sense of belonging interrupted all thoughts of popularity and cheerleading. Whatever concerns I had about my body were temporarily shelved as I allowed myself to be swept away by the generous love of Abuela Meche and the rest of my family. Whereas I had been dreading the trip, it was hard to imagine our vacation coming to an end, harder still to wrap my head around being far from my Mexican roots, from the unique smell of *pura tierra mojada* that greeted me each morning.

My entire family piled into multiple taxis to see us off. Never had I imagined that our vacation would end with all of us standing inside the airport, crying openly and hugging each other tightly, our promises to write to each other and send pictures the only way to alleviate the sorrow of saying goodbye. The sadness was unbearable. It was the first time that I felt the pain of separation from people I love, from a space in which I felt accepted simply for sharing the same bloodlines.

Abuela Meche held me for a long time and whispered into my ear. "*Cuídate siempre, mija*. Be a good daughter, and listen to your mami, okay? She works so hard for you and your brother." She let me go, and I wiped the tears from my face. "*Sí*, Abuela Meche, I will try to be a good daughter."

Mami hugged Abuela Meche for an even longer time, sobbing openly and making me cry even more because I wasn't used to seeing Mami so vulnerable. "*Ay, mamá,*" she said, "I am going to miss you so much. I don't know when I'll see you again." Abuela Meche pulled away and quickly wiped her eyes, as though allowing herself to cry had been a terrible idea. "*Sí, mija, yo sé*. But your duty is to your husband and your home, *así que* stop crying. *Ándale,* the plane is waiting for you."

Mami said nothing as we boarded the plane, her head bowed as she wiped the tears running down her face with a tissue. We buckled into our seats, and I looked over at her, at this generous *mamá* who never said anything about how much she missed her country or her family. I wondered how she handled being so far away from her loved ones, wondered if in between laundry and cooking and cleaning and assuming all the duties of a loyal wife she caught herself wishing for a different life, one in which she didn't have to be so understanding and accommodating and self-sacrificing, one in which she didn't always have to put others first.

I was too young to understand the factors that had influenced Mami's decisions, but my naivete certainly didn't stop me from making a decision for myself, my choice as solid as the plane on which we were flying.

It would be nice to have a boyfriend, I thought, *but I will never get married and have children,* a simple proclamation that I tucked into a corner of my mind, my teenage brain then refocusing on the next most important thing in the world: high school.

POM POM NIGHTMARE

LONG BEFORE I SET FOOT IN SOUTHWEST MIAMI HIGH School, Beverly Cleary and cable television had already filled my head with ideas about the magic of high school, visions in which I lost myself on the flight home from Mexico to help me forget about my sadness. I imagined myself waving pom poms and cheering at football games and pep rallies, pictured a dreamy *gringo* boyfriend complete with blond hair and big blue eyes leaning into the locker next to mine, a sweater draped over his shoulders as he offers to carry my books or give me a ride home in his convertible car, my imagination so strong that in these dreams, I, too, was a white American girl.

The plane landed in Miami a few hours later, but my head stayed in the clouds for days, my *Pretty in Pink* Molly Ringwald fantasy going strong as the bus pulled up to school on the first day.

With butterflies in my stomach and hopeful expectation, I stepped off the bus wearing my cheerleading uniform, my eyes searching for my future *gringo* boyfriend and landing instead on a black Camaro IROC-Z lowered all the way to the ground backing in to a parking space next to a blue Pontiac Fiero, the bass line of "Body Mechanic" by Quadrant Six pumping loudly from the speakers, my senses on high alert as I took in the scene before me: dark haired girls and boys in small clusters talking and laughing, snippets of their conversation landing in my ears as I made my way through the parking lot, "I told Jose *que* we would *hangear* after school, *pero* like I don't know *porque supposably* he has a girlfriend who goes to

Coral Park, *una sucia, pero* whatever, I'm totally over it," and my head coming down from the clouds *porque* this was Miami, folks, not Beverly Hills.

The student population of SW Miami High was predominantly white, but Latinos had a very strong presence, the influx of Cubans who had arrived in the sixties and seventies having lent a particular flavor to the neighborhood, our presence so unapologetic that the school had two parking lots: the American parking lot and the Cuban parking lot, a separation that confused me because my identity-in-progress was stuck somewhere in the middle, making it hard to choose a place in this new social structure. A product of Cuban, Spanish, Mexican, and Aztec Indian blood lines, my features set me apart from the many black haired-dark eyed beauties in the Cuban parking lot; neither did I look like the blond haired, blue eyed girls in the American lot. Whereas I'd never really questioned or contemplated my identity, too soon I was caught in an identity-in-crisis, the purple and white colors of my cheerleader uniform only adding to this clash of identities.

I'd spent hours dreaming about pom poms, pep rallies, and football games, had spent most of the summer stretching my legs in the hopes that I would finally be able to do a perfect split, but in reality, my body with its sturdy hips and strong legs had not been created for repetitive movements that involved leaving the earth and lifting my legs into a straddle split jump.

Physical challenges aside, I struggled to adapt to my new identity. For so long I'd pictured myself as a bubbly cheerleader with the world at her feet, had believed I would welcome with open arms the attention and the status that came with being part of the "in" crowd, but rather than embrace my new life, I retreated, the many eyes on me during pep rallies and football games feeding the fear that my every move would be scrutinized and assessed for rumor potential. I worried people would talk about me behind my back. "How did she make the squad? She's kind of weird and she can't even do a split."

Constantly worried that I was a target of rumors and gossip, it baffled me to no end that girls I didn't know would stop me in the halls to say hello, as though we'd been friends for all eternity:

"Hiiii! You look great today, and I love your hair."

"I love that shirt! Where's your next class?"

"Oh my God, I love your earrings! Come on, let's walk together."

I questioned often their motivation for wanting to talk to me, wondered if they'd do the same if I wasn't one of the girls on the basketball court who screamed at the top of her lungs and helped get the crowd all worked up for the football game we'd inevitably lose because our team sucked.

My heart hammering in my chest, I'd wonder what to say, how to act, when to laugh, how to *be*, this awkwardness worse than anything I'd ever felt. Rather than slip easily into new friendships and expand my social circle, I hesitated, tidal waves of self-doubt toppling me whenever I felt pressured to participate in any kind of conversation, be it about make-up or boys or clothes or who was dating who. Around girls I didn't know, I stumbled, their easygoing nature and relaxed attitude in no way able to silence my inner voice. *Don't say anything stupid. Don't laugh so loud. Stop fidgeting so much. Don't ask stupid questions. Stop being a dork.* My insecurity standing in the way of any meaningful connection, I doubted my every move from start to finish, at times breaking down each interaction long after it was over. *Did I say the right thing? Did I laugh at the right time? They must think I am so weird.*

Given the amount of attention I'd once received for mastering Beethoven on a recital stage, I should have felt comfortable with the recognition, but it made me uneasy. Feeling the pressure of having to be "on" all the time, I worried that not smiling or laughing enough, not fitting perfectly into the mold of a popular cheerleader would therefore banish me to the outskirts of our high school kingdom, in which every person seemed to have a place and a role to fulfill. It was even more important that I remain fully committed to being skinny at all times, there being absolutely no room for a chunky cheerleader on the squad.

Before long, I was seriously doubting my future as a cheerleader, having dropped into splits enough times to make me wonder if I'd destroyed Mami's hopes for my virginity, but rather than quit right away, I stuck to it, hoping I'd convince myself and everyone else that I loved being a cheerleader and the popularity attached to it.

"*Mija,* how do you like *los cheerleaders*?" Mami and I were hanging wet laundry on a clothing line in the back-yard, our functional dryer having been ignored for years because Mami liked the neighbors to get a good look at our underwear.

An expert at sniffing out lies, I avoided meeting her gaze. "It's great, Mami. Super fun!"

She clipped a pair of Papi's Fruit of the Loom under-wear to the line. "*Pero,* how is it? How is this cheerleader *deporte*?"

I held one of Mami's enormous bras in my hands. "*Bueno*, we cheer for the kids who play sports, *como* football *y* basketball."

She persisted. "*A ver,* show me. *¿Cómo es?*"

"Really? Okay, *mira.*" I handed her the bra and took a few steps back, nervous as I performed daggers and clasps, low Vs and high Vs, and a toe touch that nearly killed me, my performance ending with a loud "*GO EAGLES!*" that scared our dog Spanky and sent him running to a corner of the yard. "What do you think?" I said.

Mami's remarkable poker face gave nothing away. "*Bueno, mija, está interesante, muy curioso,*" which was code for *What the hell was that?* She gave me a knowing look. "Are you happy, *mija? ¿Te gusta de verdad?* Tell me the truth."

"Yes, Mami, I love it!" I said, because being popular had also made me one hell of a liar.

Pretending to be a happy, bubbly *on top of the world* cheerleader made me feel like an imposter, and my inability to accept my dissatisfaction provoked an endless stream of negative thoughts directed at no one but myself: *What's wrong with you? Isn't this what you wanted? Why can't you be happy?* Night after night I asked myself these questions and not being able to answer them, I wondered if maybe I was weird or strange or crazy or stupid or possibly all of the above.

But then *food.*

Krispy Kreme donuts during first period, a bag of ranch flavored popcorn during third period, two slices of pizza and a Coke from the food truck parked across the street for lunch, a box of peanut M&Ms right before cheerleading practice, my fear of gaining weight promptly silenced by the extra laps I ran after practice. At dinner-time, I impulsively overate *ropa vieja, arroz blanco, and platanos maduros,* my heart racing and stomach in knots a few hours later as I tossed and turned in bed, plagued by thoughts about my weird-strange-crazy-stupid self.

I had a few close friends that I'd known since elementary school, but I hesitated to reach out to them; I feared they would echo my thoughts, worried they would tell me I was indeed a weirdo for not wanting to be super popular.

Selenia was the first to broach the subject as we made our way to class. "So how do you like being a cheerleader?" We'd been friends since the third grade, when her Puerto Rican family moved to Miami from New York. We'd grown apart over the years, but I still considered her a loyal friend. By the time we got to class, she'd gotten an earful about how I really felt.

"You should join Chorus with me for next year! Dr. Willoughby is so nice, and I don't know, maybe you can play the piano, too."

Relieved she hadn't accused me of being weird, I smiled. "Really? Chorus? What would I have to do? Is it a club?"

"No, it's a class, and you have to audition. Like, I'm a soprano, and I sing with the other sopranos. I don't know what you'd be. Maybe an alto? Anyway, it's super fun. Last year we did a few concerts, and we went to a state competition. I think you'd love it." She paused, suddenly looking doubtful. "But you can't be a cheerleader anymore because we have practice after school for concerts and competitions and stuff."

"Okay, I'll think about it."

"Don't think! Go talk to Dr. Willoughby. He's always

in the classroom, even after school."

For the rest of the day, I flirted with the idea, the prospect of being connected to music again making me happy, the thought of not being popular making me anxious. Not sure what to do, I decided to ask Papi, who was sitting on the couch watching TV.

"Papi, can I ask you question?"

"*Claro que sí, mija.*"

"Do you think I should quit the cheerleading team and join Chorus?"

Unable to pull his eyes away from the emperor penguins on the screen, he said, "*Mija,* why don't you ask your mom? I don't know anything about that."

I found my mom in the master bedroom, sitting on the edge of the bed watching a *telenovela,* totally invested in a story about a poor girl who falls in love with a wealthy *muchacho*, their relationship full of obstacles and heartache because his evil *madre* and jealous ex-girlfriend are standing in the way of their true love.

I cleared my throat to get her attention. "Mami, *¿qué piensas?* Should I quit the cheerleaders and join Chorus?"

"*¿Qué? Un momento.*" She turned down the volume. "You don't like it, do you? *Lo sabía*, I knew it."

"No, I don't like it anymore. Remember Selenia? She told me to join *el chorus.*"

"Chorus? *¿Qué es eso?*"

"It's a group that sings, Mami. It's like a music class."

"*Bueno, mija*, if you think that will make you happy, *pues, ándale.*"

She returned to her love story and I to my bedroom, the weight of the world on my shoulders because this was no easy decision. The choice between cheerleading and

Chorus felt epic and life changing, my fear of not being popular so strong that I tossed and turned all night. All the same, I decided to visit the Chorus room after school the next day, which was empty of students when I walked in.

Seated at an upright piano in the middle of the classroom, Dr. Willoughby turned to look at me. "Hello, there! May I help you?" He had thin gray hair, a light beard, and tiny spectacles.

"Uhm, my name is Yvonne, and I was just wondering, you know, how to join Chorus."

Dr. Willoughby laughed easily. "Oh great! Well, you have to audition first, but don't be nervous," he said, "it's a simple process. You ready?"

"What, like, audition right now?"

"Of course, why wait?"

"Stand on the other side of the room," he instructed. After twenty minutes of "Sing this" and "Sing that," Dr. Willoughby stood up from the piano. "Very good, very good. You have perfect pitch, my dear! Tell me, how did you hear about Chorus?"

I noticed his eyes seemed to twinkle through his glasses. "Selenia is a good friend of mine, and she told me about it."

"Oh, I see. Do you play an instrument?"

"Um, I kind of play the piano."

"Oh, goodness! This must be my lucky day. Why don't you play now? Come on, sit right here." He got up from the piano and tapped the bench.

Dr. Willoughby's enthusiasm was contagious, his smile so genuine that I lost myself in the songs I played for him. Even though we'd parted ways, piano remained my first love.

Seemingly thrilled with my performance, Dr. Willoughby gave me no choice in the matter. "Make sure you select Concert Chorus and Vocal Ensemble as your electives for next year. Oh, and you won't be able to be a cheerleader anymore, as I'm sure you know, but that's okay, right? Wouldn't you rather be in Chorus?"

It took me less than two seconds to decide because *Yes, I would rather be in an air-conditioned room with other students who like music and in the company of a joyful old man whose eyes twinkle nonstop and whose smile gives me hope that perhaps I am not a weird, crazy, strange, stupid girl after all.*

Unable to contain my happiness, I smiled. "Yes, Doctor Willoughby, I'd love to be in Chorus."

"One thing, though," the seriousness in his tone making my stomach drop. "Call me Doc."

I laughed, relieved. "Okay, Doc. See you next year."

LEGS TOO FAT! YOU TOO FAT!

MY DECISION TO FORFEIT MY POM POMS AND JOIN Chorus brought me peace of mind and dare I say it, happiness, a sense of calm that permeated all other areas of my teenage life; my grades improved, my moods stabilized, my inner voice went on break, and with Papi's blessing, I got a part-time job at Pizza Hut, my habit of asking Mami to buy me nice clothes having grown old. The first day of my junior year found me once again getting off the school bus, my cheerleader uniform replaced by a pair of stone washed Edwin Jeans and a white jean jacket, the ninety-seven percent humidity not enough to kill my sense of fashion.

Walking through the Cuban parking lot, I felt ready to embrace the magic of high school once again, the five pounds I'd gained over the summer having made no impact on my optimism until I realized that whatever peace I'd made with my body would not be enough to calm the other five hundred girls with whom I shared space in high school, their religious obsession with weight a painful reminder that my body would always be something to be scrutinized and compared.

"Oh my God, I have to lose weight."

"*Ay Dios mio, pero* I'm super fat."

"Oh my God, look at my belly! I'm super bloated."

"*Ay Dios mio,* I feel disgusting."

"Oh my God, I really want pizza, *pero no,* I can't."

"*Ay Dios mio,* Gina has the perfect body, she's super *flaca.*"

"Oh my God, Tammi lost so much weight. I'm super jealous."

The obsession with being thin and discussions about food were inescapable, ongoing discourses in which even teachers participated. Thankfully, my fellow altos and sopranos in Chorus served as a buffer, the focus of our time together not on fat or calories or on being skinny but instead on four-part harmony and on bonding with the bass and tenors. True to my word, I'd joined Concert Chorus and Vocal Ensemble, a smaller choir that had become a highly dysfunctional family of sixteen with a quirky man in charge.

Being around music brought me unadulterated joy, a happiness so great that I was able to stop obsessing so much about food and dieting. It helped that I'd heard a rumor from a girl who sat next to me in Algebra II, a rumor she'd heard from her brother's girlfriend who heard it from her cousin who heard it from some *fulanita* who said that teenagers have a secret weapon called *fast metabolism*, a concept about which I knew nothing but decided to embrace because Doritos and ice cream were too good to pass up. Once again, I dunked toasted Cuban bread into my *café con leche* on Saturday mornings and thought nothing of having pizza and a cherry slush for lunch, a Charms Blow Pop my favorite dessert.

Popularity no longer concerned me, nor did I think about it, my nomination to the "Homecoming Court" mid-year thus coming as a complete surprise because I couldn't identify with any one clique in school, not with the jocks or the stoners or the athletes, not with the Cubans or the Americans, not with the super smart or super techy or super artsy, not even with my peers in Chorus.

I did my best to be friendly with everyone, to always smile and be nice to other students regardless of their ethnicity or shape or interests or status, and I avoided situations in which I'd attract unwanted attention or spark rumors. That I was somehow considered "popular" seemed ironic, given my decision to run from the limelight rather than to it, and it validated what I thought; perceptions held some kind of power, regardless of their distance from the truth. Begrudgingly, I accepted an invitation to the homecoming dance, it then becoming a painful reminder that I was not fully comfortable in social settings in which there might be too much focus on my physical appearance.

Shockingly, I missed the regular exercise I'd gotten through cheerleading, a surprise given my love for reading and napping in an air-conditioned bedroom. Halfway through the school year, my cousin Odalys convinced Raz and me to enroll in a Japanese Karate school not far from our house. We knew very little about Japanese Karate, and we assumed it would probably involve kicking, punching, and hopefully nunchucks, our knowledge of martial arts having been based on movies starring Bruce Lee, Chuck Norris, and a dragon.

Sensei Sugimoto was a strict Japanese man who did not believe in air conditioning, in water breaks, or in the words "I can't," a drill sergeant who ran his classes with a focus on preparing students not for war, but for state, regional, and national competitions. For three hours each week, I learned to bow and say *oss*, I punched and blocked and kicked and stretched, my own limitations frustrating me as Sensei Sugimoto forced my body into weird stances that made me feel as though my hips might snap. Buckets of sweat poured out of me, and many times I woke up in pain from head to toe, but it was never enough to persuade me to quit. I stuck around, the knowledge that I was better than Raz enough to keep me motivated.

The dojo was located in Westchester, a predominantly Cuban working-class neighborhood of Miami, but many of Sensei's devoted students hailed from other parts of the city, wealthy white men and women who lived in Coral Gables or Coconut Grove, doctors and lawyers who pulled up in Mercedes Benzes and BMWs, their mannerisms and behavior unlike anything I'd ever encountered. Rather than wanting to learn more about them, I kept to myself. They were older, sophisticated, and polished in a way that intimidated me, made me unsure of myself and my stubborn hips.

In between Karate, Chorus, and my part-time job at Pizza Hut, I completed my homework, respected my parents, hung out with friends, and wrapped my arms around the magic of high school, whatever deep insecurity I felt safely buried under my smile until someone came along and exposed it in the middle of a Karate dojo.

Karate class had just ended. I had stayed behind to cool down and stretch my legs. Steven, one of the black belts in the class, was stretching not far from me.

"So how old are you, Yvonne?"

I met his eyes for a second and went back to stretching my hamstrings. "I'm sixteen."

Steven was probably in his fifties, and although he'd always been polite, his direct gaze made me uncomfortable. "You're sixteen? Wow, you seem so mature. That makes you, what, a junior in high school?"

"Yep, a junior."

"I bet you're looking forward to your senior year."

"Oh, yeah, definitely."

"High school is such a great time, but it goes by fast, so make sure you live it up!" He wiped his face with a towel, my eyes locking with his as he smirked. "So what do you want to do with your life?"

"What do you mean?"

"Well," his tone condescending, "you're a junior in high school, not a ten-year-old. You should have a plan for your life."

A plan for my life? At sixteen, I wasn't focused on what do for the next fifty years, only on what to do for the next five minutes. Caught off guard and feeling like I'd just been slapped, I threw out the first thing that came to mind. "Oh, um, I want to be a doctor."

His eyebrows shot up in obvious surprise. "Oh, really? *You?* Wow. So what schools are you looking into?"

Before I could deliver yet another lie, a fellow student saved me. "Steven, *dude*, leave her alone, she's too young for you! Come on, man, I'm starving."

Steven laughed as he stood up. "That's my cue! You better start working on that life plan, because before you know it, high school will be over. Anyway, see you later!"

Having gotten my driver's license, I drove home in Mami's car, a desire to cry suddenly overwhelming me as I replayed our two-minute conversation over and over, the condescending tone of his voice, the smirk on his face and his raised eyebrows impossible to erase from my mind. *You should have a plan for your life. You should have a plan for your life. You should have a plan for your life.* That night and for many nights afterward, I lost sleep, the realization that I did not have a plan for my life instilling in me the fear that I was doing something wrong, that I was falling behind.

Teachers soon joined the *You should have a plan* team, their lessons sprinkled with doses of reality and reminders to think about my future, plan every activity, and study nonstop for the SAT because sooner or later, everything I'd done would be assessed by a group of people with power over my academic future. Having made a promise to Papi, college was a must, but my parents knew nothing about college applications and SAT prep courses; rather than guide me on how to apply for scholarships or financial aid, Papi gave me what he believed to be sound advice. "*Mija,* figure it out. *Resuelve.*"

Doc started planting ideas in my head about auditioning for music scholarships, my blunt refusal to pursue music as a career having fallen on his deaf little ears. Hoping for some kind of guidance, I made an appointment with my school counselor, an older woman who looked at my grades and assumed I'd know what to do with the college brochures she shoved into my hand. "Here," she said, "have a look at these and let me know if you have any questions. And don't forget to register for the SAT!" Too embarrassed to admit I needed help with SAT prep and college applications, I put the stack of brochures in my locker and tried to not think about them, an impossible feat given that many of my classes were Honors classes in which getting into a good university had become a competition.

"I'm applying to Georgetown!"

"I'm applying to UM!"

"I'm applying to FSU!"

"I'm applying to Notre Dame!"

"I'm applying to NYU, Stanford, George Washington, Yale . . ."

I'd always considered myself a good student, but what with my brief stint in the tenth grade as a cheerleader and a part-time job, my grades had taken a hit and were far from perfect, slightly above average at best. I'd struggled tremendously in classes like Biology and Geometry, neither of which had interested me in the slightest, and my preoccupation with popularity and image had impaired my ability to focus on schoolwork. Neither was I heavily involved in extracurricular activities that would favor me on a college application, so that left me with "Hi, I'm a Latina part-time pizza slicer, Karate chopper, singer, and pianist with sorta good grades, and hopeful parents."

Not a chance.

Thoughts about college and my uncertain future extinguished whatever happiness and peace of mind I'd found; chest tightness, racing thoughts, and a general sense of unease ruined my mood, turning me into a grumpy, irritable teenager.

But then *food*.

Whereas the Chorus room had become my second home and my consistent happy place, Doc's twinkling eyes and the beauty of four-part harmony were no match for my level of stress and anxiety, food quickly stepping in to calm me down whenever I felt my mood spiraling out of control. Up and down an emotional roller coaster I went, from hopeful to sad to happy to anxious to confident to worried, a slice of pizza or a piece of chocolate cake the only way to get me off the ride and back on solid ground.

The five pounds I'd gained over the summer turned into ten pounds and then twelve, my body becoming an easy target for horny teenage boys who thought highlighting my weight gain was a good idea.

"Wow, Yvonne. Those jeans are looking a little tight. Your ass looks huge!"

"Hey, your boobs look enormous in that shirt."

"You really shouldn't eat that donut. Your hips are getting wide. You know what they say about Cuban girls."

This unwanted attention was a nightmare come true. These "I was only kidding" comments crushed me, devastated me, their words so hurtful that each day, I made it a point to dress in looser fitting pants and shirts, the thought of my breasts or hips drawing too much attention enough to make me want to cry. Nowhere was I safe from scrutiny, Sensei Sugimoto making it all worse by grabbing my thighs in class and shouting for everyone to hear, "No good! No good! Legs too fat! Legs too fat! You too fat!" I would feel the blood rushing to my face, and a lump forming in my throat, whatever hurt and sadness I felt completely suppressed because Sensei would've taken my tears as a sign of weakness, and I couldn't handle any more humiliation.

After class one day, Steven aka Life Plan Patrol came over to me as I cooled down and stretched. "You know, don't get too upset, he has good intentions. You've gained a lot of weight, and he's just trying to look out for you. Maybe you should go on a diet." He patted me on the head like he would a five-year-old and walked away, my hate for him so real that it made me nauseated, a level of anger that turned into hurt the minute I got in the car to drive home.

That year I became an expert at feigning happiness, especially around Mami, simply because I didn't know how to describe what I was feeling, didn't know how to say,

"I'm sad. I'm mad. I'm hurt. I'm scared." My emotions manifested as stomachaches, as tightness in my chest, as impulsive overeating, and insomnia—none of which I thought Mami would understand let alone know how to fix, so I clammed up and ate my way through the pantry.

It would become my first episode of depression, a concept about which I knew nothing because depression was just another word for laziness in my family. Gradually I lost interest in everything, stopped looking forward to Chorus and Karate, my bed and my pajamas the only things that brought me comfort and relief because the thought of wearing pants that were tight made me feel worse. Eventually, I stopped wanting to go to school.

Mami poked her head into my room one morning to make sure I was up and getting dressed. "*Mija, levántate.* It's time to get ready for school."

I was still in bed. "I don't feel good, Mami. I don't want to go to school. Can I stay home?"

In a flash she was hovering over me. "*¿Qué?* What's wrong? Are you sick?" She placed her palm on my forehead. "*Bueno*, you don't have a fever. *¿Tienes el periodo?*"

"No, Mami, it's not my period. I'm really tired. I just want to stay home."

"*Sí, mija*, okay. Do you want *un* Tylenol?"

"No, Mami, I don't need anything, I just don't feel good. I couldn't sleep."

"Do you want me to stay home with you?"

"Nuh-uh. *Yo te llamo* if I need anything, okay?"

"*Bueno.* You have my work phone number, *¿verdad?*"

I nodded.

I spent the rest of the day bouncing from relief to guilt, my thoughts hopping from *I should be in school,* to

I love my bed, to *I should be in Chorus,* to *I love my bed,* to *I shouldn't be in bed all day,* to *I shouldn't eat ice cream*— thoughts that made the elephant on my chest feel even heavier, this lack of oxygen sapping the energy out of me. I missed school at least once every week for nearly two months, Mami completely unaware that I would undress and crawl back into bed the minute she left for work. Having always been a good student and a rule follower, the front office called the house, the messages they left erased before Mami came home. The notices in the mail wound up in my backpack, and I'd rip them to shreds at school, just to be safe.

Chorus was the only class in which I felt relatively okay, but Doc noticed a change in me all the same, con- cern in his twinkling eyes as he pulled me aside and asked me if I was okay. "I'm just worried about a test," I said, poor Doc unaware that the test was on life itself.

With each passing day, I grew more angry and irrita- ble, often frustrated because I couldn't identify a singular incident that had started it all, like "I failed a test." Or "I broke up with my boyfriend." Or "I got fired from work." Neither did I know to trace it back to that moment in the dojo when I was shamed for not having a life plan, my frustration turning into despair, turning into guilt and shame and self-loathing as I berated myself for being a lazy disgrace to the Cuban culture.

Mami and Papi remained in the dark because I couldn't imagine telling my hard-working parents that I didn't feel like doing anything, couldn't fathom telling Papi that I was tired, not when he spent every single day in the sun busting his ass on a construction site; couldn't picture myself telling Mami that I'd been skipping school and staying in bed, not when she got up at 4:30 A.M. to prepare Papi's lunch and go to work and cook and clean and do laundry, her day coming to an end only after we were safely in bed.

Hell would freeze over before I told them anything.

Neither could I imagine talking to any of my friends or Chorus peers; I worried they would think I was being ridiculous and stupid; only a few months before I'd been associated with the "super cool" crowd at the homecoming dance. I knew what they saw when they looked at me: a well-dressed, polished girl with beautiful long, curly hair and golden skin who smiled for everyone and played well with others. *It won't make any sense to them*, I thought. *They won't understand why I feel like a piece of shit, and I don't want to burden them with my stuff anyway.*

With no life raft in sight, I sank further into depression, my inability to snap out of it making me grumpy and *insoportable*, Mami taking the brunt of it as I snapped at her for no reason. Isolating myself in my bedroom, I spent hours trying on different pairs of pants in the hopes that starving myself for a whole day would make all the fat on my thighs disappear and when that didn't work, I'd beat myself up for not having the energy to exercise. I'd think, *You're so lazy, you're so lazy, you're so lazy*, a donut or ice cream making me feel better for about ten minutes after which Sensei's words would haunt me: "Legs too fat! Legs too fat! You too fat! You too fat!" I skipped Karate as much as I could, my excuses to Sensei revolving around school because I couldn't tell him to shut the hell up and leave me alone; it would have been disrespectful, of course.

My part time job was the only piece of my life I dared

not interrupt. Papi had made it abundantly clear from the start that I could not, under any circumstances, call in sick or be late or slack on my responsibilities. Work ethic was everything to Papi, and the guilt I would've felt from missing work would've made me feel even worse than I already did, so I carried on slicing pizza and restocking the salad bar.

Up and down I went on an emotional roller coaster for the rest of my junior year, a month-long trip to Mexico over the summer the only thing that seemed to bring me to my senses, my cousins and Abuela Meche the antidote to the spiritual angst that plagued me. Mami and I helped them move from the tiny three-bedroom home in which they'd been crammed into a five-bedroom proper apartment on the second floor of a converted home, and their excitement to have a nicer home pacified my own misery.

That summer brought me closer to my cousins, especially Lorena, with whom I explored the city but never my own emotions or worries; discussing my problems with someone who had suffered the worst kind of loss didn't seem appropriate or fair. Two years had passed since our first trip, and I could see more clearly the sadness in her eyes, the way she stared out the window of a bus as though in search of what she'd lost: a mother, a friend, an ally, a mentor. We shied away from heavy topics, and our long peaceful walks around Guadalajara were a welcome respite from the chaos in my head until I stepped off the school bus on my first day as a senior, my thoughts in disarray, a weight on my chest, my appetite and eating habits shot to hell, and my mind trying hard to figure out what the hell to do with the college brochures I'd stuffed into a drawer in my bedroom, my eyes landing not on a *gringo* boyfriend but squinting hard, struggling to focus on the elusive life plan buried underneath the twelve extra pounds firmly attached to my stomach, my hips, and my "too fat" legs, the magic of high school long forgotten as I jumped off the emotional rollercoaster and right onto a speed train to hell, bulimia nervosa the driver.

ALL ABOARD!

"*Oye*, WE'RE GOING TO YOUR AUNT'S HOUSE TODAY. You want to come?" Mami was watching me try on clothes in my bedroom, my frustration obvious as I tried to find a pair of pants that didn't feel tight.

Angrily, I pulled off the pants and reached for another pair in my closet. "I don't know, Mami," I snapped, the thought of hanging out with my uber-critical Cuban family instantly triggering stomach cramps.

"*Ándale*," she said. "Your grandmother and aunt haven't seen you in a while."

"*Ay* Mami, but all they do is criticize me. *Que* I'm too skinny or too fat or *que* my hair is not long enough. They're super annoying."

"Shhh, *mija*, don't let your father hear you," she said, lowering her own voice a notch. "Don't pay attention to them. *No les hagas caso. Ándale*, finish getting dressed, we're leaving soon."

I considered my options. I'd been struggling the whole morning to figure out what I wanted to do that day, a decision that should have been easy but had become an impossible mission. *Should I read? Should I borrow Mami's car and drive around? Should I call Laura? Should I go to the mall? Should I watch a movie? Should I go running? Ride my bike? Write to Lorena?* That I finished getting dressed and eventually hopped in the car with my parents had less to do with any desire to see my family and more to do with wanting to get away from the rapidly changing thoughts that had made feel more restless, frustrated and irritable.

Twenty minutes later, my stomach still in knots, I

stood in front of a table loaded with an obnoxious amount of food, my heart beating a hundred miles an hour as I took in the spread of Cuban pastries filled with guava and cheese, cheap potato chips, ham croquettes, sliced Cuban bread, and beef empanadas. I wanted to grab a Styrofoam plate and load it up, but I begged myself to stay strong, reminded myself of the twelve extra pounds I needed to lose, but my body told me a different story because nothing had passed my lips in well over ten hours, and I was starving.

What if I have a little bit of chicken salad and three potato chips, I thought, *and maybe half of a cookie? How many calories would that be?*

When my aunt placed a container of *chicharrones* on the table, my mouth watered, and my stomach growled as though to protest my decision to starve. The fried pork belly was enough to push my anxiety over the edge, my commitment to dieting forgotten as I grabbed a plate and plastic silverware. Ten minutes later, I'd consumed enough food for three people, my stomach so full I couldn't take a deep breath. My pants felt two sizes too small and my bra, not wanting to be left out, began to choke my breasts.

We were in the backyard of my aunt's house, apparently celebrating life in general, because in the circus that is my Cuban family, there's no need for a birthday or baby shower or engagement; we'll come together to eat and drink and dance *sin motivo.* Loud salsa music blared out of an indoor stereo and a domino game was well underway as one by one, my relatives piled food on their plates, their ease and comfort with food not lost on me, the sound of someone slamming a domino on the table with conviction drawing my eyes away from the table for a brief moment. I took in the scene, all of my relatives seemingly in love with life as guilt consumed me for eating so much. One of my cousins laughed loudly, a smile on his face as he grabbed a ham croquette and stuffed it into his mouth and in that moment, I hated him for being so chill with food, and I regretted my decision to come to the party.

I searched for my parents, and the sight of Mami sitting at the Domino table brought me a moment of relief. A cigarette dangling from his mouth, Papi stood off to the side with my uncle, no doubt discussing how *everything was so much better in Cuba* as little kids chased each other around the yard, screaming and laughing; my sudden desire to cry was so strong that I bit the inside of my lip.

Nobody in my family could've imagined how I felt because standing before them was the seventeen-year-old *niña buena* they'd always known, the one they'd always criticized for being too fat and too skinny and too weird and too much of all the wrong things. Rather than see a tormented young lady drowning in her own thoughts, in their eyes I was a talented girl who'd finally blossomed into a pretty, confident high school senior with long curly hair and an easy smile, a girl who never worried about anything, least of all her body.

My aunt walked past me, a container of boiled yuca in her hands. "*¿Oye, ya comiste?* Did you eat? Make sure you get plenty of food, *¿me oíste?* I'm glad you gained some weight, you look so much better with some meat on you."

Her comment punched me in the stomach, making me want to scream and pull my hair out, tears of frustration springing to my eyes as I imagined all the weight I'd lost between eighth and ninth grade coming back overnight. Sitting down was not an option because I worried my pants would split and the thought of walking around was torture; everyone would wonder how on earth I got *so fat* in twenty minutes. "Incredible," I imagined them saying. "She was skinny when she got here and look at her now. She's huge. *¡Está gordísima!*"

Rather than move, I stood near the carbohydrate festival, tapping my watch and wondering if time had stopped. I imagined the food inside me expanding, my stomach inflating like a balloon, the potato chips, guava pastries, and toasted Cuban bread dissolving into fat and showing up on my legs in seconds. Unable to get a grip on my racing thoughts, I did something that made no sense: I wolfed down another guava and cheese *pastelito*, the tastiness of the pastry a ten-second distraction.

Sitting in the back seat of the car on the way home, I moaned in misery, my hands resting on my bloated stomach. I'd unbuttoned my pants and pulled the zipper down within seconds of climbing into the car. I thought about the pants I planned to wear to school the next day and wondered if they'd fit after the 10,000 calories I'd just consumed. I mentally scanned my closet, searching for a pair of pants or a skirt that might not feel so tight, but still I worried nothing would fit. *What can I do? What can I do? What can I do?* An idea popped into my head as Papi made a right turn and drove down the street in our quiet neighborhood of Southwest Miami.

"I'm going for a run!" I yelled.

Mami snapped her head around in disbelief, as though I'd just announced I grew a third breast. She shook her head. "*¿Estás loca?* It's getting dark."

"*Me duele la panza, Mami,* and running will make my stomach feel better," I said.

Confused, she squinted at me, the wheels in her head spinning as she considered whether to let me run or protect me from a serial killer. Shaking her head again, she turned around and said nothing, my heart sinking because I was hoping she would figure out my obsession with weight; Mami always the one to come to the rescue. Problem was she didn't know which part of me needed rescuing; nothing was visibly broken or bleeding, only bloated.

By the time we got home, my screwed-up brain had calculated I needed to burn at least five thousand calories, but my body felt like a big block of cement, and I couldn't imagine exercising. Knowing Mami would have a nervous breakdown if I went running by myself, I changed into comfortable pajama pants, plopped down on the couch, and continued to complain about my stomachache.

"*Pero* why did you eat so much?" Mami asked me. *Because I was so hungry,* I thought.

Papi sank into his special corner of the couch and turned on the TV, his silence an indicator that he wanted no part of my distress. He pulled a cigarette out of his soft pack of Pall Mall 100s and lit it with his Zippo, his eyes squinting as he took a long drag and slowly exhaled, his way of smoking making him look like a Cuban version of John Wayne. An old school *Cubano*, Papi could've gotten away with being hot-tempered, would've been forgiven for being *apasionado*, but he'd figured out that silence was a better way to get what he wanted, namely peace and quiet.

My physical discomfort began to ease but the fear of gaining weight squeezed my weak little mind. I was just about to go to my room and do jumping jacks when I heard Mami's voice from the kitchen.

"*Mija*, does your stomach still hurt?"

"I just feel so full."

"*Bueno*, if it bothers you that much, go to the bathroom and make yourself throw up. Maybe that will make you feel better."

My heart stopped. *What?*

That she would encourage me to *throw up on purpose* was not illogical; many times, throughout her life, her *papá* would come home drunk, his love for *cerveza* and tequila earning him the wrath of my feisty *abuelita*, who often expressed her anger and frustration with the help of a wooden broom and whatever objects she could throw. Mami would watch her *papá* throw up on purpose in an effort to sober up, to feel better, and avoid the ire of Abuela Meche.

Mami knew nothing about bulimia when she encouraged me to purge; she simply hated that one of her children was suffering, and she gave me a suggestion with the best of intentions.

But the idea made me cringe, as the sight and smell of vomit had always grossed me out. *That's disgusting!* I thought, but the idea remained, and the fear of gaining weight tempted me to contemplate sticking my finger down my throat so I could stop torturing myself, go to sleep, and be thin. Again.

The agony proved too much. I got off the couch and went to the bathroom across from my bedroom and closed the door. *Throw up?* I thought. *But how? Which finger?* I could feel my heart beating faster and the cold floor underneath my feet as I stared down at the toilet.

For a brief moment, I thought about crawling into bed with my latest book in the hopes that I'd fall asleep and forget my stomachache, this thought quickly replaced by a visual of me the next morning, angry and upset because I couldn't fit into my Guess jeans, a possibility so scary that I bent over, stuck two fingers down my throat, and gagged and coughed with no success. *This is crazy*, I thought. I persisted anyway until a slightly digested concoction of guava pastries, potato chips, chicken salad, and ham croquettes came shooting out of my mouth and into the toilet.

The smell could've taken down a small elephant, but I kept going until my stomach felt empty, until all of that nasty, scary fat was gone. No thoughts went through my mind while I purged, those ten minutes a respite from the endless thoughts and negative self-talk to which I'd become accustomed over the last year. I felt no shame or horror or fear or remorse once I finished because I felt frighteningly accomplished and free, as though the fat I'd consumed had been holding my mind and body captive and we had managed to escape. I washed my face and brushed my teeth, relief filling me from head to toe because I'd found a *solución*.

Rather than stay up reading, I fell into a deep sleep. I hopped out of bed the next morning, excited for once to look in the mirror because I was sure that I'd look much thinner than the day before. I slipped into my jeans and breathed a sigh of relief as I zipped them up and buttoned them with no problem. The girl looking back at me in the mirror smiled as she gave me a thumbs up. "Good job," she said.

And just like that, I disconnected from everything I'd ever known about myself, my feet unsteady as I proceeded down a path on which I would always feel lost.

SPEED TRAIN TO HELL

IN LESS THAN TEN MINUTES, I DESTROYED MY SEVEN-teen-year relationship with food, a love/hate dynamic to which I'd always been committed. But if dieting was a bad fight, bingeing and purging was officially the divorce, a skinny body the lover to blame.

After purging the first time, in many ways I was re-lieved, my troubles with weight gain and bloating at last resolved, because I'd discovered a way to enjoy food and get skinny. I couldn't stop smiling as I got dressed for school the next day, my old mantra reverberating in my mind as I walked out the door, *I will be skinny. I will be perfect.*

I binged and purged once or twice a week at first, something akin to logic telling me to stop, but the relief I felt afterward was too powerful. With bulimia as the driver, the road to hell was a short one, a few weeks all it took to arrive at the gates, after which my body was bent over the toilet at least two times a day, sometimes three, until I was purging all the time regardless of what I ate because I couldn't handle the thought of anything in my stomach; I purged one apple, three potato chips, a glass of orange juice.

This new relationship with food excited me, the thrill of being able to eat whatever I wanted testing the limits of my stomach as I consumed a Big Mac, Chicken McNug-gets, large fries, a milkshake, an apple pie, and a hot fudge sundae over the course of twenty minutes, my heart beat-ing wildly in my chest as I purged not ten minutes lat-er, my mind sounding an alarm, *This is not a good idea,* but unwilling to consider the consequences as I sucked in my stomach and smiled at the changes I saw in the bathroom mirror, the relationship growing stronger each time I pulled on a pair of pants and noticed how much bigger they felt.

Without the restrictions of a diet, I ran wild, spending whatever money I earned on trips to Winn-Dixie supermarket, where I'd walk up and down the aisles, overwhelmed by the many choices available to me. *Should I get a meatball sub or a turkey club at the deli? Should I eat fried chicken with macaroni and cheese, or should I get lasagna from the hot food section? Chips Ahoy or Hostess Cupcakes? Ooooooooh donuts.*

My appetite and eating habits having been volatile for years, Mami was relieved to see me filling my plate with beans and rice and grabbing a large piece of *bistec empanizado*. "How are the beans, *mija? ¿Están buenos?*"

"Oh, Mami, they're amazing." I'd shove a spoonful of tasty rice and beans into my mouth. "Can I have a little more?"

"Of course, *mija. ¿Más Coca-Cola?*"

"Yes, Mami."

Nothing about my new habit scared me, nor did any piece of it weigh on my conscience, the knowledge that the food I chewed, swallowed, and purged had been made possible by my parents' hard work and sacrifices not enough to stop me. Deep down I knew they lived for Raz and me, that our happiness and wellbeing was their number one priority, that we would never go hungry nor be without shelter. Papi's calloused hands and Mami's tired eyes were proof that they hustled morning to night not for the sake of their own happiness, but for ours, a reality I'd embraced long before I purged for the first time, a reality I then discarded because nothing remained in my stomach for longer than twenty minutes and certainly not after my rapidly thinning body garnered attention.

Sensei stopped grabbing my legs, resorting instead to slapping my thighs, "No more fat legs! No more fat you! Good, good, ha ha!" It didn't matter that I nearly passed out more than a few times, that I couldn't get through a class without having to sit down and drink water, that I was perpetually light-headed and exhausted; my legs were *fat no more,* so who cared if I had energy no more.

Boys at school piped in, their every comment, stare, smile, wink, or second of attention motivating me to keep bingeing and purging because if I *could* lose more weight, why stop?

"Hey, girl, wow, looking good. Damn!"

"Looks like someone stopped eating donuts."

"Looking mighty fine in those jeans, Yvonne."

"Did you lose weight or something?"

Dr. Willoughby, my Chorus friends, my family—everyone noticed I was losing weight, but nobody seemed alarmed by it, nor did anyone suspect that I was bingeing and purging. Bulimia nervosa was largely considered a "white girl" phenomenon, an eating disorder not too common within the Latino culture, and even if it were, nobody in their right mind would openly discuss it because "*Ay Dios mío,* what would people think?"

For a few months, my secret remained safely buried underneath my smile, my few friends unsuspecting of my rapid weight loss. Daisy and I had remained friends, but we were no longer as close. She went to Coral Park Senior High, a rival high school only a few blocks away but miles apart in teenage speak, and we didn't see each other often. I had found a new friend in Laura, an outgoing and wild *Cubanita* so completely different from me that I'd gravitated toward her in the hopes that her boldness might somehow rub off on me.

Like Daisy, Laura cared nothing about popularity and status, and she made me laugh out loud:"*Oye*, stop being such a *comemierda*." She pushed me out of my comfort zone: "*Dale chica*, let's go to Club 1235 this weekend for teen night!" She questioned every single one of my clothing choices: "No, you can't wear that shirt. Are you thinking of becoming a nun? ¡*Cámbiate!*" She teased me about being too square: "Ay, you're such a rule follower!" We were polar opposites, but I loved her to death because I admired her unapologetic, unself-conscious way of showing up in the world, envied her "I don't care what people think" approach to life. But still I couldn't share with her my dirty habit; not because I feared she would judge me, but because I knew she would not rest until she was sure I'd stopped doing it, and I was nowhere near ready to stop.

I dropped from a size eight to a six to a four, my new habit a secret I intended to keep for all eternity until a young man in my Karate class thought to investigate my weight loss. In his mid-twenties, Danny Rosenberg was one of the brown belts in class, an energetic and friendly guy with whom I had connected for reasons unknown to me. The seven-year age difference between us had not been enough to scare me away because Danny was like a long-lost Jewish brother from another mother. Whereas Steve's arrogance made me angry and frustrated, Danny's humility and sincerity always calmed me down whenever I struggled in class with *katas* and *kumite,* his way of teasing me for being "wet behind the ears" not once offending me because he seemed genuinely invested in my *mawashi geri* roundhouse kicks.

Danny had won me over long before I started to binge and purge, our unorthodox friendship having moved from inside the dojo to the parking lot, where I absorbed every word that came out of his mouth, his life experiences much like the ones I'd read about in Danielle Steele books: sleepaway summer camps, trips to Europe, a membership at Ocean Reef Yacht Club, his entire network wealthy and privileged, "I'm going on my friend's boat this weekend," his demeanor relaxed as I sat on the hood of Mami's battered Gran Prix, pretending to understand his world while oil leaked out from under the car.

Danny was quick to figure out something was wrong, even quicker to peg me after class, his eyes boring a hole into me as we stood in the parking lot, another episode of lightheadedness under my blue belt. "Please don't lie to me. I know something's wrong because you've lost a lot of weight really fast, and that can't be normal." Lying to him was impossible and at that point, I was a little worried. I'd discovered blood in my vomit more than a few times, but the idea that I might have torn something inside of me had not been enough to stop me, and that alone scared me more than anything.

Leaning against Mami's car, Danny's eyes searching for the truth in mine, I confessed. "But promise you won't tell anyone, not even my parents," a promise he said he would keep so long as I let him help me.

Things seemed to happen quickly after that, with Danny handing me some forms requiring a signature from Mami, an easy task given Mami's limited grasp of

English. Danny picked me up after school—"Come on, let's take a ride"—and with his arm around me, we walked into a beautiful office building in Coral Gables where I would meet with a therapist. "Don't worry. I'm paying for this." My heart hammered in my chest as we waited for the therapist to call us in, the whole experience overwhelming me because it was not what I'd expected when Danny offered to help me. He'd brought me some articles to read, information on the physical consequences of bulimia: *You could lose your teeth, and your kidneys could fail, and your heart could stop, and you could die from this*—dangers that I could grasp on a rational level, but emotionally, I was already too attached to being skinny.

Danny waited outside while I met with an older woman, her short gray hair and round spectacles immediately reminding me of a grandmother. In that one hour, I lied to her repeatedly—"I only do it once a week, maybe twice," and "I think I'll be okay."—the knowledge that Danny was paying for the sessions weighing on me, making me uncomfortable. Knowing that I was breaking a cardinal rule in our Latino culture only made it worse. "Never share your problems with anyone outside the family." The thought of my parents finding out made me squirm as I sat on the black leather couch.

Every week, Danny drove me to see the therapist, but the shame of seeing someone behind my parents' back became a massive barrier; I lied, "I'm okay," and lied, "I'm fine," and lied, "I don't do it anymore."

Several layers of guilt buried me for three months. I felt guilty for lying to the therapist, and I felt guilty for lying to Daniel about lying to the therapist, but I never felt guilty for lying to the one person who mattered: myself.

"Are you doing better?" he'd ask after every session.

"Yeah, definitely. She's really nice."

"Do you tell her everything?"

"Yeah, for sure. She's a good listener."

"Have you stopped doing it?"

"Of course. It's really helping me."

After three months of guilt and shame, I gathered up the courage to tell Mami, hoping she'd find a better way to help me because Mami had always been the ultimate problem solver, the person who'd always been there for me, the woman who'd once made it rain in sunny California.

"Mami?"

"*¿Sí, mija?*" She was in the kitchen making *arroz con pollo*, one of my favorites. She is Mexican, but she learned to cook Cuban food for Papi, her *pozole, enchiladas,* and *frijoles fritos* reserved only for special occasions or requests. "*Cuidado, mija,* I don't want you to get burned."

"Mami, I think I'm sick."

Her world stopped at hearing those words. She immediately put down her wooden spoon and turned to me. "*¿Qué tienes?* What's wrong? You have a fever?" She placed her hand on my forehead.

"No, Mami, it's not like that. The thing is that . . . *estoy vomitando.*"

"*¡Ay Dios mío!* Where? When? Your stomach is hurting?"

"No, Mami, *lo que pasa es que* I throw up all the time. *Todos los días.* In the bathroom. And I can't stop." Tears welled up in my eyes.

"All the time? *Pero, ¿cómo?* I don't understand, *mija,* you don't have a fever."

Tears streamed down my face. "No, Mami, I don't feel

sick like that. I eat, and then I make myself throw up, on purpose." In her eyes I searched for understanding, for a magical solution, but all I found was confusion.

She scanned my face for answers, thinking hard. "Aha, *pero* . . . why, *mija*? *¿Porqué?* You don't like my food?"

"Oh no, Mami, it has nothing to do with your food. It's because I wanted to lose weight, you know? I wanted to be *flaca,* and now I throw up so that I won't gain weight."

She searched for the right words. "*Ay Dios mío, mija. Bueno*, you have to stop, okay? *Deja de hacer eso*, okay?" She looked to me for reassurance that I would stop, because this was a problem she'd never had to solve in all her years as a mom. She had mastered cuts, bruises, fevers, tummy aches, cramps, and headaches, but throwing up on purpose hadn't been included in the *How to Be an Amazing Latino Mother* handbook.

I wiped my eyes and shrugged. "Okay, I'll try."

She sighed in relief. "*Sí, mija,* and you will feel better once you stop, *te lo prometo*." She gave me a hug and kiss and picked up the wooden spoon to stir the rice. "*Mira*," she said proudly, "look what I made, your favorite. This *arroz con pollo* will make you feel better, *mija. Tú verás.*"

She can't help me, I thought, the whole idea of bingeing/purging to get skinny too foreign a concept for her. I went to my bedroom and laid down, a sinking feeling in my stomach, the knowledge that I would find a way to purge the dinner she was making weighing heavily on me, but not enough to make me consider keeping it in my stomach. Those grains of rice, regardless of how small a portion, would mentally torture me unless I got them out of my system.

A few days later, Mami happened to catch a popular Spanish talk show, *Cristina*, a Latino version of Oprah Winfrey. The topic of the show was eating disorders. Several young ladies and their families met with a doctor who described the dangers of eating disorders and how for some, they could result in death, Mami's worst nightmare. For so long she'd been focusing on the perils of the *whole wide world*, and yet there I was tempting death in our very own bathroom.

The show made an impact on Mami because she involved Papi, their eyes flooded with concern as they sat me down and bombarded me with questions.

"How long have you been doing this?"

"Why did you start?"

"Did you tell anyone outside the family?"

"Will you stop?"

"Can you stop?"

I can't stop, I thought. Confessing to Mami had been my half-assed attempt to get help, but the minute I'd felt some extra fat on my stomach, I had binged and purged, the minute I'd started to feel anxious about my future, I'd gone to McDonald's and ordered five thousand calories worth of food and had driven to the mall to purge in a handicapped stall of the Sears bathroom. Too easy.

I looked at my parents, the two people who had been tasked with the job of making sure I was safe and loved, and I knew it was an opportunity to come clean, to be truthful, and to trust them, but Mami's sad eyes and Papi's calloused hands were reminders that they'd done more than enough for me.

So I lied.

"I'm okay, Mami," I said. "I stopped doing it already,

I promise. I felt better after I talked to you. It was just a phase, but I'm okay now, *te prometo.*"

Mami looked at Papi, who lit up a cigarette. "*¿Are you sure, mija?*" He said, squinting at me as he took a drag. "*Dime la verdad*," he said.

But the truth is terrifying and destructive, I thought. *La verdad* would destroy them because they wouldn't be able to help me, not really. There was no money for a therapist or a hospital and even if there was, I knew they wouldn't go down that path. The doctor on the show had suggested therapy, medication, and/or hospitalization as the best options, but Mami would first believe in Our God Almighty, that He alone would be responsible for my recovery. Papi would expect me to *resolver,* to figure it out, the thought of paying for a *psicólogo* out of the question because psychologists were only for "crazy people," not for good Cuban daughters with talent and smarts.

So I lied again.

"*Sí, Papi,* it's the truth. *Yo estoy bien.*" I tried to lighten the mood. "*Oye,* what are we having for dinner? Can we order pizza from Godfather's?"

Mami laughed and said, "Of course we can have pizza," perhaps choosing to believe that I would simply eat and not purge when in reality I'd drive to a gas station near the house after dinner, ask the cashier for the bathroom key, and throw up every bit of the five slices of pepperoni and mushroom pizza I'd eaten very slowly to make them believe I was fine.

But I was not fine. My face turned yellow, and I developed dark circles under my eyes that no amount of concealer could hide. On days we ate dinner as a family, I'd eat a normal amount of food and then sneak off to my bedroom, my heart racing as I stuffed my face with brownies and cookies and potato chips I had stashed under my bed. Afterward I would tell Mami that I needed to shower, and lock the bathroom door for privacy, a huge no-no in Latino culture because God forbid I fall and crack my head open.

Sometimes I'd find Mami standing outside the bathroom door, making pretend she happened to be walking by on her way to their bedroom. She'd kiss me on the cheek, lingering for a few extra seconds to see if she could catch a whiff of vomit. She would walk into the bathroom and scan the area, looking for signs of *arroz con pollo* or *picadillo*, never finding anything because I'd become an expert at cleaning every inch of the bathroom and my body, eliminating all evidence.

"*Mija*, did you vomit?" She'd say, her eyes scanning me from head to toe.

"No, Mami, of course not! Believe me."

She'd sigh. "*Bueno*, I think *Diosito* is hearing my prayers, but I'm going to keep asking Him to help you, *por si las moscas*."

Mami's eternal faith in God and Papi's enduring faith in me kept them from doing what most *Americanos* would have done: gotten professional help. But their faith wasn't enough to save me from the hell in which I found myself, an inferno in which not having a plan for my life scared me, not being able to fulfill my promise to Papi shamed me, and not knowing what I wanted to *be* other than skinny worried me, emotions I managed by bingeing and purging morning, noon, and night.

ROAD TRIPPING

HAVING WON THE PARENT LOTTERY, I ENDED UP IN A home with two people who had the right amount of patience, self-control, and compassion, for without the combination of all three, Raz and I might have had all of our teeth smacked out of our mouths before we reached adulthood. These qualities coupled with their ability to provide food, shelter, and safety might have been enough for me had I not been born with an abnormal level of curiosity, with a burning desire to explore more deeply what I saw, heard, and felt. More than patience, self-control, and compassion, I needed from my parents a willingness to answer every single one of my questions—all of which usually began with one word: Why?

Mami and Papi were easily the two people with whom my curiosity was able to flourish. Mami would answer my questions readily, as though she'd been waiting all her life to be on my talk show. "Mami, why do you wear orange lipstick? Why orange and not blue?" Papi, too, was a good sport. He smiled when I questioned his way of making *cafecito,* laughed when I wondered out loud why he had fake teeth.

By the time I'd entered high school, they had patiently answered hundreds of questions about their lives, their honest answers stored in my brain as information that would later provide me with a deeper understanding of who they had been before they'd become hard working immigrants in America, before they'd become parents, before they'd had a chubby and curious daughter who questioned their tradition of roasting a pig in a *caja china* every Christmas Eve.

His twenty-third year on earth forever marked by disappointment and fear, Papi chose to leave the life he'd always known in Güira de Melena, Cuba, shortly after Castro rose to power in 1959. He dared not breathe a word of his plans to his three brothers, two sisters, and parents, as Committees for the Defense of the Revolution had been established in every corner and crevice of Cuba. Tasked with being the "eyes and ears of the revolution," these neighborhood organizations reported any kind of activity that smelled of dissidence, and rather than assume his family members could be trusted, he kept his plans to himself.

Papi hopped onto a "borrowed" boat in the middle of the night with five other young men in 1961, his faith not so much in God but in himself and in the unknown waters ahead of them, which he hoped would guide them to safety. With little time to plan and pack supplies and nobody onboard who knew anything about navigating the sea, they ran out of gas, their food supply dwindling to nothing. Drifting west and then south for nearly a week, they survived by sharing the little bit of water they'd been able to save, their prayers answered when a Honduran fishing vessel spotted them and brought them to safety. They traveled through Mexico and were granted entry into the United States as political refugees.

After arriving in the US, out of gratitude he joined the US Army and served for two years, an honorable discharge to his name as he returned to Los Angeles. He took the first job that did not require a formal education because he did not sail away from Cuba with a college education in his pocket; he'd attended school for only three years, during which he'd learned the basics of reading, writing, and arithmetic. He found a place to live. He connected with other Cubans who had defected to the US because Cubans have a way of finding each other no matter where they are in the world.

After several unsuccessful attempts by the CIA to assassinate Castro, Papi came to accept that the bearded terror and his *revolución* were in it for the long haul, and it would take his family a few more years to realize they, too, would be better off in the United States. His sister Leya and her children came to the US in 1966. The Mariel Boat Lift in 1980 brought his parents and his special needs brother, Onelio. In 1984, his younger brother Pipe and his family boarded a plane for Panama, where they would spend a few days before flying to America, Papi and the rest of the family having gathered enough money to sponsor them into the United States. Eventually, all but one of Papi's siblings would make the trip to America, everyone settling into the North American capital of Cuba: *Miami*.

As a child, I loved asking Papi about his life and his journey to America, the sadness in his eyes often lost on me, my innocence preventing me from recognizing that his story came from a deep well of pain buried beneath the strong body and gentle demeanor that made me feel safe and loved.

Mami, on the other hand, was not fleeing a dictator when she stepped onto a train departing from Guadalajara, Mexico in the early hours of a spring morning. In fact, she hadn't wanted to leave Mexico at all. Abuela Meche had insisted she live in California for six months, hoping Mami would rethink her decision to marry the young man to whom she was engaged, as Abuela Meche and everyone in the *barrio* knew he was *un borracho*.

Mami did not cross the Rio Grande with the help of a coyote or travel with a caravan of immigrants across the border. With a six-month tourist visa in her hand, Mami was driven across the border by my Tio Armando and my mom's sister, Tia Esperanza.

For the first few weeks, Mami cried every night, homesickness wrapping itself around her, this being the first time she'd ever been away from her family, the silence in her sister's home too much to bear because she worried nonstop about her siblings and feared her fiancé would find another girl to marry. This torturous silence came to an end after Tia Esperanza helped Mami get a job at a clothing factory in downtown Los Angeles, whatever relief she felt at being able to send money to her family eclipsed by the fear of being caught by *la migra*, for as much as she missed home, she couldn't help but appreciate the soothing hot water on her skin as she showered, couldn't deny how good it felt to have a bed to herself, let alone her own room, couldn't help but feel the slightest bit of satisfaction whenever she counted the money she'd set aside for herself, the idea that she had her own *dinero* a concept so foreign that it overwhelmed her.

She worried incessantly that *la migra* would raid the factory and send her back to Mexico, a terrible nightmare about these men in dark suits prompting her to look over her shoulder one morning as she walked into the coffee shop on the ground floor of Campus Casuals, her eyes scanning the room in search of her captors and connecting instead with the eyes of a handsome young man from Cuba who wasted no time in getting to know her.

Mami and Papi decided to get married only a few

months into their relationship, any thoughts about marrying the *borracho* back home gone from Mami's mind, for in Papi she'd found a man who made her feel safe and loved, a man who spoke a different dialect of Spanish, drank a weird version of coffee, and who couldn't dance to save his life, but Mami was willing to accept their trivial differences for the sake of love. Mami sent a letter to Mexico asking her parents for permission to marry this nice Cuban man, Papi then notifying his family that he would be marrying a *Mejicana*, their union made official by the Catholic church on a sunny day in February, because even though Papi had wanted to get married at the courthouse, Mami had been adamant that she and her virginity would not be handed over to Papi by anyone other than God.

In spite of their work ethic and strong value system, the challenges at times would seem insurmountable. There existed no concrete path to success, no guarantee any of their combined efforts would someday pay off, both having emigrated to a country with zero knowledge of the language, the culture, the customs, the rules, the laws. Yet their heavily accented English and limited knowledge of US laws would not be enough to stop them from having children, not enough to prevent them from believing that they, like millions of other people, deserved a place in a country in which rather than survive, their children would thrive.

Their limitations would not deter them from hoping and believing that our lives would be better in Miami, their lack of education never an obstacle because they were willing to work for the sake of survival rather than fulfillment, their accomplishments a testament to the determination of immigrants who arrive in the US with not a God damn penny to their name, hoping to make a life in a country that does not always welcome them.

As a child, it was hard for me to wrap my head around how they'd managed to survive. Mami and Papi's ability to read and write *in Spanish* was limited, their grasp of English even more so.

"We always figured things out, because we didn't have a choice, *mija*," Papi once said to me. "Someday you will understand what it means to make *sacrificios*."

But I understood nothing about sacrifices on the day of high school graduation. Mami and Papi had always provided for us and made sure our basic needs were met. Their determination to give us a better life had paved the way for piano lessons and cheerleading and Chorus and even Chinese food, but I appreciated none of it as I faced my bedroom mirror wearing a cap and gown, sweat pouring out of my armpits like a broken water fountain.

An ongoing preoccupation with my physical appearance and an episode of depression during my junior year had hurt my grades and any chance of securing admission to a good university, not that I'd spent any time filling out applications. Dr. Willoughby had driven me to auditions he'd coordinated in secret because no matter how much I'd resisted or complained or threatened to not show up, Doc had refused to let my talent go to waste. His efforts and my talent had secured a partial music scholarship to Florida International University. My only other choice was Miami-Dade Community College.

Still, I should have been happy to have choices. I should have been happy with the chance to get educated beyond high school. I should have been thrilled with the opportunity to go where none of my family members had ever gone: to a salaried job with good health benefits and a retirement plan.

But I was not happy, not even a little bit.

No part of me escaped my jacked up *nervios* as I walked on stage to receive my high school diploma. I lamented the fact that I hadn't binged and purged that morning because surely that would've made everything better. After the ceremony, my peers gave each other high fives while I stood around fighting waves of nausea and worrying the fountain of sweat under my gown would result in an embarrassing puddle around my feet.

I avoided eye contact as I made my way toward my family because answering questions about my future made me want to stab my eye with a fork. Nobody could have guessed I was paralyzed with fear or that I was *freaking the hell out*. As I stood for pictures with family and friends, I heard snippets of conversations all around me about who was going to FSU or UF or Ohio State or George Washington.

And where was I going? To Red Lobster for dinner and then maybe FIU.

We crammed into a booth to celebrate the occasion, and I tried to be normal, tried to enjoy my shrimp scampi with no thought to calories or grams of fat; feigned happiness when a waiter brought out a complimentary dessert as a celebration gift. On the way home, I thought about what someone "normal" would do after eating two thousand-plus calories. Watch TV? *Boring*. Go for a walk? *Too hot outside, and I feel like a whale*. Crawl into bed and read the latest Danielle Steele book about white people problems? *Okay, maybe*. Instead, I borrowed Mami's car under the pretext that I was going to a graduation party and drove to the corner gas station, where I purged shrimp scampi, six bread rolls, Sprite, chocolate cake, and vanilla ice cream in the bathroom.

So much for normalcy.

I handed the bathroom key to the gas station attendant and felt compelled to explain why I'd been in the bathroom for fifteen minutes. "Thank you so much," I said. "Something got stuck in my teeth and it took me forever to get it out. *So* frustrating!" He took the key and said nothing. *He must know what I've been doing for the past six months,* I thought. I scratched the gas station off my list of safe places to purge.

Mami's car smelled like Pall Mall cigarettes, the seats worn out from years of piano lessons and baseball games and family outings to visit our Cuban relatives. I drove around Southwest Miami for over an hour to make it look like I'd actually gone somewhere with friends. Papi was already in bed when I walked in the door, and Mami was exactly where I thought I'd find her: on the couch watching a horror movie.

Apparently, her childhood hadn't been horrifying enough.

"How was it, *mija*? Did you have fun at the party?" she asked me without so much as looking my way.

I started to tell her about the imaginary party. She paid attention until a man holding a chainsaw burst onto the TV screen. "*¡Ay Dios mío!*" she screamed. "*¡Córrele!* Run, *¡pendeja!*" I left her watching *Texas Chainsaw Massacre*, which was just as well because I wanted to sleep and forget about my own life massacre, which would scare the shit out of me the next morning.

After dinner the next day, Mami, Papi, and I went

for a walk around the block, a family ritual because Papi insisted a post-dinner walk helped his digestion. It was more a way for him to fart unapologetically, the sounds embarrassing us from start to finish, the smell killing a few plants along the way.

Papi spoke up a few minutes after we started our walk. "*Mija*, wait," he said. Knowing his gases would take us down, Mami and I always walked a few steps ahead. "I want to ask you something."

I slowed down. "*¿Qué pasa*, Papi?"

"*Mija*, let's talk about your graduation present."

Caught off guard, I looked at Mami, who raised her eyebrows and shrugged. "What do you mean?" I asked. I hadn't expected anything beyond my celebration dinner and the necklace and earrings Mami had bought me from Avon.

"*Ay*, Papi, forget about that. You don't have to give me anything." And I meant it. Sort of.

"No, no, *mija. A ver*, what would you like?"

"*Bueno*, I don't know." I placed a hand on his shoulder. "Let me think about it while we walk."

Fighting off mammoth-sized mosquitos, I contemplated what I wanted while considering their financial situation. A car was out of the question, this I knew for sure, and I didn't need or want clothes. *What would be fun?* I thought.

We turned the corner, and the sight of bougainvillea at our neighbor's house immediately reminded me of California, which reminded me of my cousins, which reminded me of childhood, which took me right back to my favorite memories, which distracted me from any thoughts about a graduation gift.

Images began to appear one by one on the movie screen of my mind, complete with sounds and smells: road trips with our cousins down to Baja California, all of us crammed into Tio Armando's van, the pungent smell of the ocean as we opened the windows, a brief stop at *La Bufadora* in Ensenada for a glimpse at a blow hole where Papi always lifted me up so I could see the water shooting from the earth with ferocious intensity; my cousins and I running away from the crashing waves at Rosarito Beach, hungry seagulls flying all around us as we laughed and shrieked each time the cold water swallowed us, our blue lips trembling as we sucked on *paletas* and walked back to the van.

The snow-capped mountains in the distance whenever Papi took a left onto Delmar Avenue, our final destination a trip to Big Bear to see snow for the first time, Raz and I struggling to walk through ten inches of snow with improper footwear while Mami poured hot chocolate from a mug; our road trips to Cachuma Lake and Yosemite Park, where we'd spend the day wading in the rivers, learning how to fish; the many times Papi drove us out to Santa Monica Beach or Redondo Beach, Raz and I hunkered down on the sand, digging furiously for sand crabs with which we did nothing except throw them back in the ocean.

I recalled our week-long road trip from L.A. to Miami, how much fun it had been even though we'd driven our parents absolutely crazy, their patience, sanity, and cigarettes nearly gone by the time my father parked our 1974 Caprice Classic in front of Sergio's Café on Bird Road on Thanksgiving Day, 1978.

It dawned on me that our road trips had come to an

end after we'd moved to Miami. The unforgiveable hot Florida sun that bore into Papi on construction sites had quickly worn him out, and Mami dared not drive on *el freeway* because her *nervios* would not allow it. From the day we'd arrived in Miami to my senior year in high school, the furthest we'd ever traveled as a family was to Hialeah, a mere ten miles from our home in Southwest Miami, and Hialeah was not what you'd call a *destination*.

An idea began to take shape in my mind. I took a deep breath. "Papi, I think I know what I want."

"*A ver,* tell me."

"Let's go on a road trip." Papi's eyebrows shot up in surprise. "*Mira,*" I said, the plan materializing faster than I could speak, "we can drive from Miami all the way to Guadalajara. Yeah!" I was brimming with excitement and speaking rapidly, afraid the idea would vanish before I voiced it. "We can stop in New Orleans, in Texas, maybe explore parts of Northern Mexico. We can stay in cheap motels, you know, like the ones we stayed in when we came from California!" Papi looked down as we walked, deep in thought. "I can help with the driving because I have a license. What do you think?" I held my breath.

He remained quiet, which gave me hope because I knew he was contemplating the idea. We stopped at a neighbor's house, because Papi loved to scope out yard-work and gardens, forever commenting on the way flowers or plants were growing and noticing which ones needed water or plant food. He was such a *guajiro*.

Papi looked at Mami. "*¿Qué piensas, Hilda?* You'd like to see your family, no?"

Mami had been pacing and stopped. "*Ay Dios mío,* I don't know. How many days would it take?"

Papi did the calculations in his head. "Five to six days, I think."

"*Y el carro*, will it make it? It's not exactly a new car."

"*Vaya*, you have a point." He paused, thinking things over. "*Bueno*, I can sell my pick-up truck and buy a van, which we can sell in Mexico for a profit. We'll fly back and with the extra money, I will buy another pick-up, a nicer *camioneta*." He smiled broadly. "I like the idea."

Buy a van? Make a profit? I thought. "Where did that come from?"

He tilted his head back and laughed. "*Mija, soy Cubano*. We are always trying to make more money." He paused. "¡*Bueno, vámonos!* Let's do it."

I hugged Papi and kissed him on both cheeks. Mami went into panic mode and muttered *Ay Dios mío* the whole way home, no doubt praying we wouldn't crash or get kidnapped by a UFO or contract a deadly disease along the way.

The excitement of a road trip distracted me from thoughts about the rest of my life, giving me a break from anxiety. Bingeing and purging took a back seat while I helped Papi find a van that wouldn't leave us stranded in a small town in Mississippi where my people might not be welcome.

We planned to leave at the end of June and return after one week in Guadalajara because any more time off would've resulted in a financial crisis; neither of my parents had paid time off. My secret habit had depleted a lot of the cash I'd saved from my part-time job, but I wanted to contribute all the same. Papi accepted my offer to help pay for gas and food along the way. Raz chose to stay behind because he was working at Publix Supermarket, and

Going to college didn't scare me. Depression may have stolen my energy and motivation for a solid year, but it had not destroyed my passion for the smell of fresh paper, sharpened pencils, brand new textbooks. No matter that my grades had slipped, deep down I knew I was a smart person and that I loved being intellectually stimulated and challenged.

But the decision about what to *be* for the rest of my life stopped my heart, it being the one test question for which I'd forgotten to prepare. Enrolling in college meant I'd have to choose between doctor or dentist or lawyer or accountant or teacher or nurse—white-collar professions my parents had encouraged me to pursue since I'd crushed my chances of becoming a concert pianist, these being the only careers of which we knew outside of housekeeping/labor/food service jobs. Sooner or later, I would have to be *Doctora* Castañeda or a cashier at Pizza Hut.

Right on cue, my heart started pounding, my palms got sweaty. I stopped folding clothes and sat down on my bed, trying to calm down, trying to stop my thoughts from going down a well-traveled path in my mind. But one thought led to another thought which led to multiple thoughts—all of which made me more anxious.

What if I never figure it out? What if I have to work at Pizza Hut for the rest of my life? Oh my God, no, but what else can I do? I don't want to be a doctor; I hate going to the dentist. And I'm not smart enough to be a lawyer, but they look so cool on TV and so smart. But only white people become lawyers because I've never met a Latino lawyer, actually I've never seen a Latino doctor except in telenovelas, and they're always men, so maybe I should focus on getting married and having a family. Yeah, that would probably be he had fallen head over heels in love with *una Americana*.

I was in my bedroom picking out clothes to take on our trip, each outfit carefully selected to make me look and feel as skinny as possible, God forbid I look chunky as we drove through Alabama. As I pulled clothes from my closet and threw them on my bed, I dreamed about the many stops we would make along the way to Mexico, pictured beautiful sunsets against the backdrop of charming small towns and rolling hills that stretched for miles, visions based not on my experiences but on what I'd read or seen in movies.

Mami came into my room and snapped me back to reality. "*Mija, estás* excited about going to *el* college?"

Damn it, I thought. I was not excited about *el* college and in zero mood to discuss it. I concentrated on folding the clothes I'd chosen for the trip. "Oh yeah, Mami, of course. It's going to be so fun, so different." One look at her and she would know I was lying, what with her Mami radar.

She picked up a T-shirt and folded it. "*Qué bueno, mija*. We are so proud of you."

Guilt, sadness, and shame overwhelmed me, making my eyes water. Being an imposter was tough business. I turned to search my closet for something so that I wouldn't have to look at her. "Aw, thanks, Mami."

"I can't wait to tell your *abuelita* you're going to college. She is going to be so proud, *ay Dios mío*."

When all she got from me was, "Uh-huh," she left. My heart sank when she closed the door. Daydreaming about our road trip became futile because thoughts about the *rest of my life* showed up and once again held my brain hostage, demanding a decision on the rest of my life as ransom.

the right thing to do, but I can't imagine being a housewife and taking orders and serving a man and raising kids. But I love kids so much, and maybe I should think about having kids someday, but why do I need to have kids? Hello, I'm only seventeen years old, but if I wait too long then I'll never have a family. But do I really want a family? What should I do? What should I pick? What should I be? Life sucks.

I thought trying on different outfits would distract me. Big mistake. I hadn't purged in a few days nor exercised, so everything felt tight, constricting, too much a reminder that I was probably gaining weight. My heart started to beat even faster, and my nerves felt frayed from overwhelming anxiety and fear.

But then . . . *food.*

I reached underneath my bed for my junk food stash and quickly stuffed two Hostess CupCakes into my mouth, followed by Twinkies and a bag of Doritos—all of which I washed down with a can of warm Coke. From there it was a quick trip to the bathroom to purge. Five minutes later, my face washed and teeth brushed, I calmly strolled into the kitchen as though nothing had happened and helped Mami put dinner on the table.

I binged again. Laughed. Binged some more. Smiled. Waited for Mami and Papi to go for a walk without me so I could purge. Washed my face, brushed my teeth for the second time in two hours. Drank three glasses of water with two Ex-Lax and felt a little better. Tried to get some sleep. Failed. Got up at one in the morning and drank NyQuil. Crashed.

This pattern repeated itself many times before our trip, and I wondered if I'd be able to sneak inside a bathroom without Mami following me, worried I wouldn't be able to get away with bingeing and purging. The thought of eating and not being able to purge scared me, so I stocked up on Ex-Lax, which I'd started taking as a secondary measure to purge everything in my system. I packed extra bags of David's Sunflower Seeds and a box of Blow Pops, hoping these "safe foods" would keep my urges to binge and purge in check.

We watched the sunrise as we drove out of Miami. My mom sat in one of the comfy swivel chairs in the back and I in the passenger seat with a bag of sunflower seeds in my lap, more than ready for our adventure and hoping it would be every bit as fun as I'd imagined. We drove through Florida, Alabama, Mississippi, Louisiana, and finally Texas and just as before, we stayed in cheap motels along the way. I helped Papi with the driving whenever he felt tired, which wasn't often, the few times I was able to take the wheel and cruise along a stretch of highway making me feel whole in a way I'd never felt.

We didn't have cell phones or GPS back then, just an old map that Papi had referenced to get us from L.A. to Miami only ten years prior. Each time we stopped in a new city or town, I took charge of translating and gathering whatever information was needed.

"How much farther to the next gas station?"

"Is there a hotel up ahead?"

"Where can we get a good breakfast?"

"Do you sell sunflower seeds?"

All along the southern belt of the United States, we were met with friendliness and generosity at each pit stop, helped by complete strangers who willingly answered my questions about their small town, their families, their lives because I couldn't walk into a gas station to ask for directions or sit down for breakfast at a diner without engaging someone in conversation. Gone was the intimidated high schooler who'd shied away from conversation with strangers; on the road I felt liberated from the high school kingdom in which I'd been trapped and hungry for something new in which to sink my teeth. From each encounter I took something away, a little nugget of information that I stored away in my developing brain—a new way of looking at people, a new perspective on the country in which I had been raised. I noticed the unique ways in which people spoke, loved the way they smiled at us warmly whenever we sat down to eat, their accents different from one state to the next. "Hi, can I get y'all somethin' to drink?"

With each mile logged, my brain seemed to expand and grow, my soul reaching for something I couldn't name back then, a budding awareness of myself as a citizen of the whole world taking root in my young mind.

We picked up two of my uncles across the border of Laredo, Texas; they'd made the trip to help us navigate through Mexico all the way to Guadalajara because we were coming from *El Otro Lado* with Florida license plates, and Papi wasn't sure just how safe it was. But danger was not on the forefront of my mind as we snaked our way down to Guadalajara; I was wrapped up in staring out the window for hours, my mind focused not on how I looked or what I ate but on the changing landscape as we inched south, lushness and mountains replacing the arid northern Mexico desert.

Exactly six days later, we parked in front of my grandmother's home in downtown Guadalajara, the sun setting in the distance as Papi climbed out of the van and lit up a cigarette. My little cousin Mario peeked out of one of the windows and yelled for everyone to hear, "*¡Ya llegaron!* They're here, they're here!" Mami's enormous family came outside to welcome us with open arms and with no shortage of love and excitement. Everyone pitched in to help us unload the van and bring our suitcases upstairs. It felt so good to be around my cousins and family, to be on Mexican soil, so much so that when my cousin Lorena asked me how long we were staying, I turned to her and said, "Hopefully forever."

When Papi asked me to call the airline and book our flight home one week later, I realized immediately that I had no intention of leaving, no desire to go home and go to college and do what everyone else my age would be doing. Staying behind wasn't something I'd planned from the start, but rather a logical consequence of being on the road for six days, during which I'd discovered a profound sense of freedom and a desire to wrap my skinny arms around the magical uncertainty of each day. Going to college not knowing what I wanted to study or what I wanted to "be" felt much like putting an end to my journey of discovery, a journey that I couldn't imagine doing anywhere else but in *Mejico lindo*.

"Papi, I need to talk to you." I had found him smoking a cigarette in front of the apartment with my Tio Miguel.

"*Sí, mija. ¿Qué pasa?*

"I don't want to go home. I want to stay here with Abuela Meche and my cousins."

"Did you ask your mother?"

"No, I thought I would ask you first, because she would tell me to ask you anyway."

He nodded. "You're right about that. *Bueno*, are you

sure you want to stay, *mija*?"

"Definitely! I love it here. What do you think? Can I stay?"

To my surprise, Papi nodded slowly and said, "*Bueno, está bien*. If you want to stay, it's okay with me, but make sure you check with your grandmother and cousins." His blessing completely invalidated my assumption that straying too far from home was unacceptable, what with me being a good Cuban daughter. I shouldn't have been surprised, as Papi had proven to be a rebel of sorts, not one to fit the mold of a typical Cuban father who wouldn't let his precious daughter out of his sight. "And be careful, eh? When you're ready to come home, *me llamas.*"

"Really? You're not mad? What about college?"

He shook his head. "No, I'm not mad, but I do want you to go to college. If you want to stay a few more weeks, it's okay. I know your *abuela* won't let anything bad happen to you. You have money, right?"

I had three-hundred dollars to my name, a small fortune. "I think I have enough. I'll try to not spend it all at once." Which wouldn't happen unless I bought *taquitos al pastor* for the entire neighborhood.

"*Está bien*. Obey your grandmother, eh? Make sure you help her with whatever she needs, and be nice to your cousins."

"I will, Papi, I promise."

"Oh, and one last thing, don't go sticking your nose in their problems or arguments, okay? You're nobody to give them advice because you don't know their lives, and it's none of your business. You understand?"

I nodded and ran back up upstairs to tell Lorena the news.

Papi gave me his blessing assuming I'd want to come home in a few weeks, but Mami's *nervios* sensed differently, igniting her tear ducts. Mami and I had never been separated for any great length of time. On the one occasion she'd let me spend the night at Jeannine Decker's house across the street, I'd only been able to stay for a short while, the pang of sadness I had felt at being separated from Mami not worth a whole night of discomfort during which I would feel grossly out of place and awkward as well as terrified to wake up with no eyebrows or with a permanent magic marker moustache. I'd heard horror stories about slumber parties, and although I'd been tempted to try my hand at giggling and gossiping and being normal, in the end I told Mrs. Decker that I wanted to go home.

When Mami opened the door, she had been surprised to find me standing there, pillow and pajamas in hand. "*¿Qué pasó, mija?* Why are you here?"

"I don't know. I just wanted to come home. I missed you."

When Mami heard I was staying in Mexico, she started to cry, weakening my resolve. But I wanted to prove to Papi and myself that I could manage a little bit of freedom, that I could *resolver* like he'd always taught me, that I could be strong and independent, that I knew exactly what I was doing.

I assumed it was okay to stay with my huge family in their not-so-huge home. I hadn't considered the fact that a) there was no extra bed, b) I would be another mouth to feed, and c) I was essentially useless. Mami hadn't taught me to cook or to do any cleaning, God forbid I damage one of my talented piano hands. The only thing I had to offer my family in Mexico was a roundhouse kick to a burglar in the middle of the night.

But if my family thought it strange that I'd chosen to stay, they kept their thoughts to themselves. They shifted bodies so that I could sleep in one of the small rooms next to the kitchen on one of two twin beds, the other one occupied by Tio Javier, little Carlitos, and little Mario.

In a matter of days, I was settled into the home with Abuela Meche and twelve of my relatives: Tio Javier, who was diagnosed with paranoid schizophrenia and heavily medicated, two aunts (one a single mother), seven *primas*, two *primos,* and a sassy Cocker Spaniel. Chaos ruled every second of the day what with everyone's school and work schedules, giving me the freedom to observe and reflect and learn.

For the first few nights, my body tingled in anticipation for the next day and the next, knowing each one would bring a new experience and with it, another chance to explore and broaden my mind. I felt like a world traveler, an adventurer, a citizen of the world. For the first time since my junior year, I felt emotionally and mentally stable, happy, at peace. I believed in my heart that I'd left my fears and insecurity behind, that I'd dropped them somewhere on the border between the US and Mexico.

But in the words of Confucius: No matter where you go, there you are.

A BROKEN COMPASS

CRAMMED INTO THE BACK SEAT OF A CAR WITH NO tablets or cell phones or anything electronic to distract us, Raz and I had gotten into many fights when we'd made the long drive from L.A. to Miami.

"Maaaaaaami," I'd say, "tell Raz to stop looking at me. He's looking at me! Make him stop!"

I was no angel; I, too, had enjoyed driving Raz crazy. "Maaaaaaami," Raz would yell, "Yvonne took my yellow crayon, and I was using it! Ugh, she's such a pain!"

On that journey of three-thousand miles, not once did Papi raise his voice, lose his cool, or hit the dashboard in a rage; instead, Papi would light up a cigarette and take a long drag, the smoke seeping out of his nostrils like a magic trick. Mami would grab the cigarette right out of his mouth and take not one but three drags in a hurry, *puff blow, puff blow, puff blow.*

"*Ay Dios mío, estos chiquillos* are driving me crazy!"

In the third grade, I learned that cigarettes could kill our parents, a fact that scared me to such a degree that I turned to my older brother for help. For once, Raz and I agreed on something; we decided we both hated their smoking habit, our daily fights over who got the biggest slice of pizza or what to watch on our one television coming to a halt as we came together to save our parents' lungs.

"We need to hide their carton of cigarettes," Raz said. We were in his bedroom playing *Asteroids* on our Atari gaming system and miraculously getting along.

"That's a great idea! But where?"

"I know!" he said. "In your piano bench!"

"But it's crammed with sheet music."

"Who cares? You can move some of it, right? Put it in your bedroom or something."

"Oh, yeah! Good idea."

"Come on, let's do it now." We dropped our Atari joysticks and went to work. Impressing my big brother was a priority, so I quickly moved Rachmaninoff, Bach, and Mozart into my bedroom and slid them under my bed. We grabbed their carton of cigarettes from a drawer in the kitchen, placed it in the piano bench on top of Chopin, and covered it with Beethoven.

We watched and giggled as both Papi and Mami opened every drawer in the kitchen in search of their prized carton of cigarettes.

Papi checked the same drawer for a third time, nostrils flaring like an enraged bull. "I left them right here, *¡coño!*"

Mami started to wring her hands. "*Ay Dios mío, pero* where did I put them?"

Mami was notorious for putting things away and then forgetting where, exactly, she put them. Kneeling on the couch, Raz and I watched the drama unfold from the living room, our smirks a dead giveaway that we were up to something. One look at our faces was enough to send Mami to the bedroom to grab one of her skinny, faux leather belts, our mission coming to an end as we handed them the carton of cigarettes lest we get the beating of a lifetime.

Note to my eight-year-old self: Never hide cigarettes from people who decide whether or not you live.

"But it's so gross," I said to Raz, disappointed yet relieved we'd escaped death. "Cigarettes are super nasty! I hate them! I am *never* going to smoke!"

Nine years later and living in Mexico I would eat my

words because of anxiety. Because of depression. Because of existential angst.

Never say never.

I'd been in Mexico for a few weeks, the initial excitement having worn off only to be replaced by a nagging feeling in the pit of my stomach that I'd made a mistake. I was watching my Tia Yolanda, recently home from her job at a department store, as she dove into her evening ritual. Sitting on the couch, her shoes abandoned somewhere near the front door, she peeled off her knee-high panty hose and removed her fake eyelashes at the same time, a skill I found fascinating. Lovingly she massaged her feet, her hands then moving up to massage her neck as she asked everyone about their day, quick to laugh at everyone's trivial stories and always finding my ramblings particularly funny. "*Así que* you helped Meche find her dentures, and they were in the fridge? *Válgame Dios.*"

After ten minutes of self-care, Tia Yolanda grabbed her pack of Montana cigarettes and pulled one out, her manicured hands tapping it on the box and lighting it with a match. Like someone examining a piece of art, I stared as she took a long drag and blew out the smoke, her eyes closing and body falling back into the battered cushions, a smile on her face—a picture of relaxation and peace that I wanted badly to purchase.

She looks like a sophisticated actress from a 1940s movie, I thought.

Wanting the peace that oozed out of my aunt with each drag, I grabbed her pack of cigarettes and took one out. Holding it to my nose, I closed my eyes and sniffed it, the smell reminding me of Mami and Papi and making me homesick.

Tia Yolanda sat up. "*Oye*, what are you doing?"

"*Tia*, can I try one? I just want to see what it's like."

She sighed. "*Ay, mija*, I don't know. Your parents would be very upset, *¿no crees?*"

"*Tia*, they both smoke, like, a lot. I probably won't like it, but I just want to try because you look so relaxed when you smoke. *Ándale*, just one time."

"Let her, Yolanda," Abuela Meche piped in. "One cigarette won't kill her."

Meche had smoked for fifty-plus years, quitting only when Tio Ramon threatened to jump off the roof of the house. I was surprised at her willingness to let me experiment, her vote of confidence enough to convince Tia Yolanda. "*Bueno, pues*. Don't tell your Mami, okay? And make sure your Tio Ramon doesn't find out."

"I won't, I promise. But how do you do it? Can you show me?"

"Like this." She grabbed a cigarette and held it close to her cherry red lips. "*Mira*, you put the tip in your mouth, inhale a little bit, and then blow it out." I did as she told, my desire to look glamorous mocked by the instant choking and coughing it produced, the effects of nicotine hitting me two seconds later and making me feel less stupid. *Oooooh*, I thought. I felt good. Mature. Worldly.

Later the same evening, I sat on the front stoop with Lorena. We were lost in conversation when our Tio Miguel showed up with a six pack of Sol beer. He slipped one into my hand and winked. "Have a beer, *mija*. *Ándale*." I cracked it open, took a few sips, and then passed it to Lorena. For a brief moment, I wondered what Papi would say if he knew I was drinking beer.

Papi was not a heavy drinker, not one to pour himself

a stiff one after work. On special occasions, he would drink a brownish liquid on ice that he referred to as, "*Yohnny Wocker en las rocas.*" The one time I'd taken a sip by mistake, I had choked and sputtered, Papi tilting his head back to laugh, perhaps relieved that I hated the taste of hard liquor. Not once had I ever seen my father drunk and unruly, his only habit a cold bottle of Coors with a sandwich on Saturday afternoons after yard work.

Papi introduced me to alcohol by pouring me a quarter glass of beer to go with my own Serrano ham and gouda cheese sandwich just after my thirteenth birthday.

"Drink to enjoy the moment, *mija*, not to get *borracha*," he'd said, as I took small sips of the yellow liquid. "When you drink too much, the next day you won't feel good. *¿Me oíste?*"

I had nodded, pretending to understand. "*Sí,* Papi, okay."

Papi had been trying to normalize drinking, to instill in me the concept of moderation and responsibility. Not really understanding what he'd meant, I had agreed to obey him because beer tasted funny to me and who'd want to drink that awful *Yohnny Wocker* anyway.

As I got older, Papi continued to give me cryptic advice when it came to alcohol. When I was fifteen years old, he gave me permission to go to my first high school party with Raz, and had reminded me again that he trusted me to know right from wrong. Excited for my first real party, I'd chosen to wear what I'd considered super racy: shoes with a heel, a denim miniskirt, and a white sheer blouse. Mami had helped me put on mascara, pink lipstick, and a hint of blush for my cheeks.

"Wow, sis, looking good." Raz poked his head into my

bedroom as I'd stood in front of the mirror, second-guessing my outfit.

"Really? You think so? It's okay? I don't look like a skank?"

He chuckled. "No way, not even a little bit. You look cute."

"Thanks, Raz! I'm almost ready."

"I'll go outside and wait in the car."

I checked myself a few more times in the mirror, suddenly unsure of what Papi would say about my outfit. Holding my breath, I tiptoed toward the front door, trying not to make any noise. My hand was on the doorknob and freedom was within reach when I heard Papi shout from the living room. "*¡Yvonne!* Come here, please."

Damn it. I walked to the living room and stood off to the side, out of his view. "*¿Sí,* Papi?"

He turned around and smiled as he gave me the once over. "Wow, *mija,* you look *bonita.*" *Whew,* I thought. "*Pero,* come here," he said, tapping the space next to him. "Sit down, I want to talk to you."

I sat down, trying to keep my skirt from riding up my thighs.

He turned down the volume on the TV, adopting that slow, methodical, and painful way of speaking that he used when lecturing us. Nervously, I looked at the clock, worried his lecture would last an hour.

"*Mija,*" he said, after he took a long drag on a cigarette, "I want you to pay close attention to what I say to you." I nodded. "*Mira*, when you get to *la fiesta*, find *un muchacho* you're not attracted to, okay? *Dile* 'hello.' Talk with him for a few minutes, hm? And then walk away."

I paused to let it sink in, not sure if I heard correctly.

"Um, okay. Why, though?"

"Ah, *porque* when that *muchacho* starts to look good, tell your brother *que* you need to come home." He winked at me. "*Así de fácil.*"

I'd let out a nervous giggle. "That's it?"

"That's it," he said, a funny smile on his face as though he'd just told me the secret to life. "*Mi niña*, be safe. Have a good time."

I got in the car, the A/C on full blast and Def Leppard playing at an unreasonable volume. "What the hell was taking you so long? We gotta go!" Not one to have patience, Raz backed out of the driveway and put his foot to the pedal.

"That was super weird," I said, my armpits already sweating from the one-hundred percent humidity as I strapped on the seat belt.

"What happened?"

"Papi told me to find a guy I'm not attracted to when we get to the party. Isn't that bizarre?"

"Say what?"

"Yeah," I shrugged, "and that when that guy starts to look good to me, I need to tell you to bring me home."

Raz hit the brakes and howled, clapping his hands. "That is AWESOME!"

"What did he mean?" I said, grateful that I put on my seat belt. "Did I miss something?"

Raz laughed so hard he actually snorted. "You sure did, but you'll figure it out sooner or later. Just come and find me when you need to go, okay?"

In very little time I decoded Papi's advice because after two wine coolers, I was attracted to every single guy at the party, and wanted to kiss and hug everyone. Before I did anything stupid or embarrassing, Raz grabbed me by the arm and led me out the door.

Relentless in his mission to keep me from making poor choices, Papi continued to drop hints about the consequences of drinking too much. I occasionally went to parties with Raz and continued to drink wine coolers, which helped me feel less self-conscious and more comfortable around my peers, but I was always too afraid to get stupid drunk because the last thing I wanted was to disappoint *El Jefe*.

But I was alive and well in the birthplace of tequila and *micheladas* with no job, no schoolwork, no Chorus practice, no Karate, no responsibilities, no clue. Anxiety, depression, and a full-blown eating disorder had busted my moral compass, and with no parental supervision, the temptation to run wild had never been stronger.

Papi is not here, I thought, *but I'll do what he said, drink to have a good time.*

I finished the beer and asked Tio Miguel for another one as I ran upstairs to get a cigarette from Tia Yolanda. I put the cigarette in my mouth and noticed Tio Miguel shaking his head and laughing. *"Ay yay yay, mija*, you better hope your parents don't find out." He took the cigarette from me and took a drag.

Combining alcohol and nicotine made me certain I'd never felt better in my whole life. What a buzz! What a high!

Lorena shook her head. "Ay, Yvonne, you are so crazy. I can't believe you're smoking. Aren't your parents going to be upset?"

I shrugged because in that moment, I told myself I didn't care what anyone thought. Two beers and a cigarette later, I felt *free*. I felt like an *adult*.

We went inside and sat in the living room, where I continued to drink and smoke and laugh and talk, until I began to slur and lose the ability to stand up straight. I passed out on the couch, but not before I gave every person and animal in the house a sloppy hug and kiss and told them how much I loved them.

The next morning, I couldn't remember anything and had that horrible sinking feeling that I'd done something wrong. Papi had told me to drink in moderation, and I'd ignored his advice. Tio Miguel walked into the living room as I struggled to get off the couch.

"I have such a headache, *Tio*," I said, expecting him to scold me for getting drunk. I rubbed my temples with my fingers.

He laughed. "I have the best cure, *mija*, don't worry."

"Oh, yeah?" I expected a couple of aspirin, but he put a cold beer in my hand.

"Here, drink this," he said.

My stomach did a somersault, but Tio Miguel encouraged me to take a few sips, promising I would feel better. Against my better judgment, I took the beer from him, and after a few sips, the nausea and headache began to wane. *Wow*, I thought, *Tio Miguel is a genius*.

And so, it began.

I started buying my own cigarettes and beer and looked forward to my daily happy hour, because it was when I felt liberated from my *nervios*. After a few beers, I didn't think about how much I missed home, didn't think about college or the rest of my life, didn't feel sad or worried or anxious. Under the influence, I was far more social: funnier, smarter, sweeter, more loving, more generous.

And definitely more curious.

"*Abuela*, how old were you when you had your first baby?" We were in the kitchen peeling carrots and potatoes and getting the *frijoles* ready for *la comida*.

"I was fourteen, *mija*."

"Fourteen? That's crazy! Why did you start so young?"

"Because *tu abuelo me robó* when I was thirteen."

"My grandfather kidnapped you?"

She laughed. "*Bueno,* that's what people used to say whenever someone ran off with a boy. *Pero no te creas*, I loved him."

"*¿Y entonces?* What happened?"

"*Pues* we got married and had more kids."

I couldn't imagine having kids and being married at fourteen years old, especially when I'd only stopped playing with Barbies at age twelve. "Weren't you scared?"

"No, *mija*, I wasn't scared, *y menos mal* we got married young because my poor Filiberto died at fifty-three years old."

"How did he die?"

She pretended to drink from a bottle. "*La botella, mija.* He was an alcoholic."

I felt a pang of guilt for drinking around my grandmother, wondered if she was disappointed in me. "I'm sorry, Abuela, that must have been so hard."

"*Ni modo, mija*," she said, as though she'd just announced the sky was blue. "I had to keep going. I didn't have a choice." She grabbed my hand and squeezed it. "*Mija,* only God knows why things happen the way they do. All you can do is be strong and keep going, *seguir adelante*."

I wasn't sure in which direction I needed to *seguir adelante* so I focused on a routine. My new habits alleviated my *nervios*, which helped me cut back on bingeing and purging. My diet consisted of sunflower seeds, candy, and coffee, along with a few more items added to my "safe foods" list: chicken soup broth and fresh fruit smoothies. Each morning I would walk to the *mercado* with Abuela Meche, spend time with her while she made *la comida*, and then I'd work on a jigsaw puzzle or read until everyone else got home. Sometimes I would go for a walk by myself around La Plaza Tapatia or Mercado San Juan De Dios.

Knowing that I could look forward to my daily happy hour kept my mood stable, kept it from slipping too far into dangerous territory like the unknown future. As soon as most everyone was home, I'd drink a few beers to get in a better mood, one that made my relatives laugh and smile, one that made me feel at peace and worry free.

But I couldn't out-drink, out-smoke, or out-smart whatever was plaguing me, because I would still wake up in the middle of the night and toss and turn for hours, trying to stop the endless and disjointed flow of thoughts that gave me no peace, most of which had to do with the rest of my life.

Innocently I had assumed being far from home and free to ponder life's greatest questions would boost my confidence, make me strong, help me *find myself*. But the self I found once the novelty of drinking and smoking wore off was still confused about what to do with her life, because her doubts and fears had followed her straight across the border.

I grew more antsy with each passing day.

Abuela Meche suggested I visit some of the *pueblos* outside of Guadalajara, sensing my restlessness. My grandmother was nothing like Mami; she never mentioned her *nervios* or worried I would catch pneumonia if I walked outside with my hair soaking wet. She encouraged me to take day trips and explore more of Mexico, fully believing I would figure things out if anything went wrong.

She sent me on day trips, her eyes warm as she gave me detailed instructions on which bus to take, where to hop off, and what to look for in each village. She encouraged me to bring food just in case I got hungry on the bus, and I never had the heart to tell her that I wouldn't eat it, that each time she put a sandwich in my bag, the temptation to eat it and purge would consume me until I was able to give it away, which made me feel guilty.

Leaving the safety of my grandmother's home should have terrified me, but getting a chance to visit new places filled me with nervous anticipation and eliminated all thoughts about the rest of my life.

I'd look out the window of the bus as it traveled down dirt roads toward villages like Tonalá, Ocotlán, and Tlaquepaque. Seeing how other people lived in these small villages humbled me and continued to expand my perspective of the world. Once again, I was overwhelmed by the freedom I felt looking out the window of our van as we cruised through the southern United States and down through Mexico. On those long stretches of road between Miami and Guadalajara, wanderlust seeped into my spirit and solidified a love for exploration and discovery. Being on the road and learning about the world resonated in me; it was an unmistakable high I never got from beer or cigarettes or bingeing and purging. I couldn't have known then how much my curiosity about the world and about people would dictate the course of my life—and in many ways, save me.

KEEPING SECRETS

I'VE MET A LOT OF DIFFERENT PEOPLE IN MY LIFE, PEOPLE who've challenged me and enlightened me with thoughts radically different from mine. I've engaged in heated discussions about political ideologies, immigration laws, and the First Amendment, each time learning something new about myself and about others. Difficult experiences have encouraged me to question my own implicit biases and explore my beliefs as a Latina growing up in America. I am beyond grateful for every person with whom I have interacted because I firmly believe we have the capacity to learn from each other, whether directly or indirectly.

My whole life, with its many ups and downs, has been a series of interactions with teachers and mentors, my father the best teacher and mentor I've ever had, the person to whom I refer when I am searching for answers, the man who helped me lay the foundation for my core beliefs and helped me solidify my value system.

These days I remember him wearing his *guajiro* hat and heavy white sneakers that supported his weak ankles and tired feet, his belly pushing through a plain T-shirt with a pocket for his cigarettes and always a twinkle in his eye, words of wisdom at the ready for anyone seeking guidance because Papi held a PhD in Life.

No matter the topic, Papi always had something to offer, some tidbit of information he'd picked up. He was an expert on construction matters, be it how to lay Italian tile, put up drywall, paint a house, build a shed—his knowledge complimented by a hodgepodge of information: mating rituals in the animal kingdom, World War

II, the history of chess, gardening. He'd learned a great deal from his own life experiences, but he loved his books and television shows.

With the advent of cable television, daily we fought over what to watch, because Raz loved fishing shows, and I liked movies about underdogs climbing their way to victory. Raz and I would fight for power of the gigantic remote control until Papi sat on the couch and lit up a cigarette, code for "Give me the remote control, *coño.*"

With impressive patience, Papi would go through all the channels until he found something educational, usually on The Discovery Channel. We'd sit quietly and pretend to be interested in giraffes or hippos, all the while hoping Papi would fall asleep so we could watch MTV, the only channel on which Raz and I could agree.

Many Sunday mornings during childhood, I would stumble into the kitchen and find Papi sitting at the dining room table with a plate of scrambled eggs and bacon, diligently reading *El Miami Herald* front to back and drinking *cafecito.* Sunday was the only day he'd be showered and clean shaven for more than a few hours because during the week he'd walk in the door covered in soot or paint or dust or fiberglass, his plain T-shirt soaked in sweat. He would set down his Igloo and Thermos and take the cold glass of water Mami handed him. He'd gulp it down, kiss Mami on the cheek, and say, "*Bueno*, time to shower."

Whenever I practiced the piano, Papi would sit on the velvet green couch and read thick hardcover books about the history of this or that country, eyebrows joined together in deep concentration. Where he got these books remains a mystery because he'd never join me and Mami on our many trips to Westchester Public Library. He'd take a break from reading to say a few words whenever I paused between songs. "Very good, *mija,* very, very good."

He rarely raised his voice, and Lord knows we certainly pushed his buttons, because Raz and I argued over everything: toys, the last donut, the weather forecast. When we hid his dentures and put Mami's gigantic rollers in his hair while he napped on the couch, Papi laughed along with us because his "normal" was calm and patient.

But when it came to politics, Papi was another man altogether. His passion for *la política* often led to heated discussions with the many *amigos* he'd made over the years, fellow *Cubanos* he knew at the barber shop, at Sedanos Supermarket, at the local bakery. He would leave the house on Saturday mornings and return a few hours later, his voice raspy from shouting and his body drenched in sweat, enough fire in his eyes to set the house ablaze.

Growing up in L.A., we'd been surrounded by my mom's Mexican family, where our budding identity had been rooted in *frijoles fritos, tortillas, la Virgen de la Guadalupe,* in uncles who usually drank too much and got into fights during family gatherings at my Tia Lancho's house in Rosemead. The absence of Mexican relatives in Miami paved the way for indoctrination into all things Cuban. *Frijoles fritos* were swapped for *frijoles negros*; freshly baked *conchas* were switched out for toasted Cuban bread; *la Virgen de la Guadalupe* was more or less replaced by *la Santa Barbara.*

Shortly after we moved to Miami, Papi started taking us on field trips to *Calle Ocho* on Sunday mornings. Many of the *Cubanos* who'd defected to Miami congregated outside of small cafes along the strip of road that ran through

Little Havana, hard-working men and women who talked about how the sun and the moon and the stars and
literally everything within the universe was much, much
better in Cuba, but Miami would do for the time being.
On these excursions, we came to realize that the father
we'd always known was simply a cover for another wildly
passionate and vocal man, one with a whole other version
of Spanish.

Raz and I had learned to speak Spanish before we'd
learned English, my father having insisted that we speak
it in the house, completely ignoring everyone's advice that
we assimilate into *los Estados Unidos*. He'd remind us often that being able to speak two languages would help us
in the long run, optimistically ignoring the discrimination and racism so often associated with the Latino culture and instead choosing to believe that being bilingual
was a plus, not a negative.

Imagine that.

Our relatives in California having dominated so
much of our upbringing, we had learned a Mexican dialect of Spanish, which is different from Cuban Spanish or
Salvadoran Spanish or Puerto Rican Spanish or Domini-
can Spanish. Papi's version came to life once we moved to
Miami, perhaps a consequence of finding so many people
from his original tribe gathered in one place. At first, I
thought it was a completely different language, what with
sentences flying out of Papi's mouth at lightning speed,
most of the words chopped in half, valuable consonants
dropped as though he couldn't be bothered with that *s* or
r.

Words and phrases to which we'd grown accustomed
disappeared in a flash, common phrases like *ándale* and

híjole, only to be replaced by *vaya* and *qué barbaridad* and *le ronca el mango,* this new language making me question how well I knew Papi.

On those Sunday morning field trips, Papi's favorite topic of debate was Cuba's tormented relationship with the United States. The calm, patient father we'd always known would vanish the minute it was mentioned, his participation in the conversation a whole-body endeavor; arms would flail, a hand would slam the counter, hips would thrust as he shouted rather than spoke in this wild new language; neck veins would bulge, nostrils would flare, his eyes would nearly pop out of his head, and smoke seemed to come out of his ears whenever the discussion led to *ese Presidente Kennedy* and the mess he'd made of a bay full of pigs.

Like Papi, the other *Cubanos* would shout entire sentences at everyone and no one at the same time, the noise inside the café almost unbearable, their fingers pointing toward the sky as though to hold God accountable for the fate of Cuba.

"*Ese Castro* is a *comunista*, ¡*coño*! ¡*Los demócratas son una mierda*! Castro can kiss my *culo*!"

At first, I worried they were actually fighting and that Papi would somehow get hurt, my chubby little body relaxing only at the sight of one of them putting his arm around Papi and saying, "*Coño, chico*, you are so right." Although way too young to understand their conversations, I managed to learn that a) Papi was well liked, and b) Castro was not.

Papi had been making a statement on those mornings, perhaps giving voice to his sense of self-worth, for no one in particular but himself.

The raised voice: "I have something to offer."

The arms flailing: "I have an opinion."

The hand slamming a counter: "I have a voice."

The finger pointing toward the sky: "I have perspective."

The fist pounding on the chest: "*Coño*, I have value."

All his life, Papi refused to be an uneducated immigrant with a limited mindset. He devoured newspapers and books and sat engrossed in documentaries because his brain, much like his body, had needed sustenance and fuel for growth. Learning more about the world never led to a job promotion, but that had never been his goal. At his core, he was genuinely curious, a bona fide scholar.

Meanwhile, fresh out of high school and roaming around Mexico, I was genuinely unmotivated, a bona fide *slacker*. Five months had gone by, and I was still drifting, in search of something I couldn't name but hoping to convince myself that I was having the time of my life.

I was in the kitchen with Abuela Meche, helping her make *pozole*, a traditional Mexican stew with hominy and pork. I'd casually mentioned to her how much I loved *pozole*, and she'd decided to make it, believing I was a normal person who consumed solid foods and never purged.

As I stirred the stew, I considered opening up to Abuela Meche about my struggles with food and weight, but I recalled one of my last conversations with Mami, and it was enough to give me pause.

"*Por favor, mija*, don't even consider telling Lorena or your Abuela Meche about your problem, okay?" I had been helping Mami pack her suitcase the day before their flight back to Miami.

I bristled. "Huh? What do you mean?"

She whispered, "I just don't want them to know that you were, em, *tú sabes, vomitando*. What will they think?" She shook her head. "*Qué verguenza.*"

Wow, I thought. *She's ashamed of me.* "But it's the truth, Mami."

"*Yo sé, pero* if you tell them, the rest of the family will hear about it, and then everyone will know. *No, mija, por favor,* don't say anything."

The blood drained from my face, and I felt like I'd been punched in the stomach, so visceral was my reaction. I shouldn't have been surprised. Mami had always been worried about what people would think or say when it came to just about everything we did. She'd always been quick to make sure we looked and acted like the ideal Latino family, whether in church or at the grocery store, because *what would people think* if we were anything less than perfect.

But I'd never imagined she would be ashamed of me, had never thought she would ask me to hide my truth. Tears had sprung to my eyes as different emotions overwhelmed me—anger, hurt, confusion, sadness, guilt. Not wanting to argue with her, I nodded. "Okay, I won't say anything."

Our conversation played in my mind as I watched Abuela Meche pouring love into the *pozole*, the realization that I couldn't open up to her hitting me hard. There was nobody in my family to whom I could talk, and my only confidante, Daniel, was back in Miami and probably assumed I was okay. But in reality, I would eat a few bowls of *pozole* and later purge every kernel of hominy, a truth that caused an avalanche of loneliness to swallow me.

No, I thought. *Don't cry. Don't cry. Don't cry.*

We left the stew to simmer. I sat down at the kitchen table with a beer to keep me company, watching as Abuela Meche moved around the small space, wired to stay in motion at all times. She had the body and hands of a woman who'd spent her entire life in a state of perpetual sacrifice and hard work, her face lined with deep wrinkles and age spots, her skin the color of honey. Abuela Meche's skinny arms had carried eighteen children at one point or another and her breasts sagged from years of breast feeding and, like my father, she, too, had lost nearly all of her teeth.

But she moved like she'd long ago given the world the middle finger, like she'd made a decision to give it her best shot, her every ounce of energy, every drop of sweat, destiny be damned. Watching her in action, living the life she was given with not an ounce of bitterness in spite of all the turmoil, starvation, and poverty brought me a sense of comfort, reminded me that we were descendants of the Aztecs and capable of anything.

But in that moment, the Aztecs had nothing on the strength of my emotions.

Don't cry, don't cry, don't cry, I begged myself. *You need to be just like her. Una chingona. A warrior.* A sip of beer calmed me down.

Abuela Meche was at the sink washing dishes, her back to me. "*Oye, mija,*" she said, "how long do you think you'll stay here in *Mejico?*"

Not once had she ever asked me about my future plans. Caught off guard, I lit up a cigarette and took a sip of beer because the future was my least favorite topic. *Puff blow sip, puff blow sip*. "I don't know, Abuela. How long do you think I should stay?"

She laughed. "*No, mija*, I can't answer that for you, *pero* don't you miss home? Don't you miss your parents?"

I shrugged like it didn't bother me one bit. "Not really, maybe a little bit." *Puff blow sip, puff blow sip. Don't cry, don't cry.*

"Why do you like it here?"

"Maybe because I'm learning new things about the world. It's sort of like being in a new school, don't you think?"

"*Sí, mija*, and you've always loved school, *¿cierto? Tu mami* told me you got into *la universidad*." She went back to stirring the *pozole*. "You know, she never got a chance to finish school because she had to work and help the family, *la pobrecita*. Your parents are so happy that you have that opportunity." I was too afraid to speak and hoped she would change the subject. When I said nothing, she said, "*¿Y entonces?* Do you think you'll go?"

I grabbed another beer out of the fridge. "It's not that I don't want to go, and you're right, I've always loved school. But college is different because I have to pick what I want to be for the rest of my life, and I don't know what to choose, so it would be a waste of time."

"And you have to choose something right away? Is that how it is?"

"Not really, but . . ." I searched for the right words and miraculously landed on the truth. "I guess I don't want to make a mistake."

She put down the wooden spoon and turned to look at me, the full force of her gaze boring into me. "*Mira, mija*, there are no guarantees in life. *Solo Dios sabe lo que hace.* You need to take risks, take chances, *no seas cobarde*. Mistakes are good for you because they make you stronger."

In which case I'm destined to be a superhero. "I guess so."

She shook her head from side to side, a knowing smile on her face. "Someday, *ya verás*, you will know what this life wants from you, but for now, you can stay here and keep me company." She paused to taste the stew. "But remember, *mija*, you are very smart and so talented. God made you that way for a reason, *¿no crees?*"

I nodded. "Maybe so."

She wiped her hands on a dish towel. "I have to go to the bathroom. Keep an eye on the *pozole, mija*."

Sleep eluded me the next few nights because even after a few beers and a shot of tequila, my mind refused to let me rest, set in motion by Abuela Meche's words to me. "Someday you will know what this life wants from you." Something picked at my brain, challenged me to explore my thoughts, to dive into my mind, but I simply didn't have the right scuba gear for deep introspection. Instead, I remained near the surface, struggling in one place, stuck in a whirlpool of the same thoughts.

What am I doing? Why am I here? What do I really want? Why do I have these thoughts? What's wrong with me? Why can't I just relax? Why can't I stop thinking? Why can't I turn off my brain?

Every night, I went up to the rooftop to smoke, the stars and the moon my loyal companions, waiting until I felt sleepy enough to go back to bed. One night, I stayed on the rooftop and watched the sunrise, my head pounding from lack of sleep and nicotine, too strung out to enjoy the beautiful colors in the sky and struggling to control my racing thoughts.

I'd spent over six months in Mexico, having assumed

it would be an extended version of our road trip, a time of exploration and learning and reflection, a way for me to figure out what I wanted to do with my life. But Mexico had become a battlefield for two sides of me wrestling for control: the good Latina daughter who worried about disappointing others and making mistakes, versus the girl who wanted the freedom to explore, the permission to drink and smoke and experiment, societal and cultural norms be damned. This raging battle had brought dire consequences; I was struggling on a daily basis with an eating disorder, using bingeing and purging to calm me down when it was too early in the day to drink.

It's no wonder I felt so lost. I couldn't decide which way to go and what to do because I wasn't yet convinced that mistakes were okay, that perfection was not necessary, and that eighteen years old was no time to figure out the rest of my life. I couldn't have known what life wanted from me because rather than think about what I would contribute to the world, I'd been wired to consider only what the world might bring to me, namely a good job with solid benefits.

The sun hit my face as I sat on the rooftop smoking a cigarette, feeling drained. I thought about what Papi might say, what he'd advise me to do.

"*Mija*," he would say, "*resuelve*. Figure it out."

I decided to go home, citing college as my reason for leaving, which everyone in my family seemed to understand. No way in hell could I tell them the truth, that I was confused and scared of disappointing everyone, because I'd gotten them used to the funny, happy, slightly intoxicated and fearless version of me.

As the plane made its way into the sky, I looked down

on the lights of the city, remembering Abuela Meche's last words to me as we hugged goodbye.

"*No tengas miedo, mija.* You are so strong. You are special, and God has a plan for you."

Too bad Abuela forgot to tell me God also has a sense of humor.

MY FAVORITE MISTAKE

WHEN I WALKED INTO TGI FRIDAYS THE DAY AFTER COMING home from Mexico to apply for a job, there was no strategy behind it, no intense conversation with my parents about my career goals, no realization on the flight home that my dream was to own a restaurant or to be a chef. The only thing I knew for certain as I filled out the application was that I had no money and nothing but time on my hands. The irony of choosing to work in a restaurant while dealing with an eating disorder completely escaped me; in my eyes, I was a high school grad with limited work experience who needed to get a job and quick, not an eighteen-year-old suffering from bulimia nervosa.

The restaurant was quiet that afternoon as one of the managers invited me to sit down for a quick interview, during which random questions were thrown at me at a rapid pace: whether or not I liked people, whether or not I could handle being on my feet for hours at a time, and "By the way, could you start tomorrow?" I accepted on the spot, no questions asked.

Papi was happy for me, proud that I had gotten a job yet quick to remind me to be a responsible and flexible employee. Much like when I got a job at Pizza Hut, he advised me to not ask too many questions or demand a higher wage, and to mind my own business at all times. "Remember, don't get involved if you see someone doing something wrong or illegal," he added, "because it will only cause you trouble, eh? *Mija*, keep your head down, and *no te metas en problemas.*"

He made it abundantly clear that I should not question

the order of things unless my life was in danger, and even then, I should think twice about opening my mouth, but I was born to a man who'd taken a dump on Castro's ideas, a man who openly voiced his opinions and thoughts, who wasn't afraid to take risks, a man who stood in the middle of a café on *Calle Ocho* with his head held high, a glaring example of courage and fearlessness.

I ignored his advice because after six months in Mexico, I felt capable of making my own decisions, my emotional and mental vulnerabilities not able to convince me otherwise. After a few weeks, I started pestering the manager to "Pretty please, let me be a waitress," having realized that being a hostess would surely bore me right into old age. I'd spent a great deal of time in Mexico with nothing but my thoughts and I wanted to expend all the physical energy that remained relatively untapped. No part of me enjoyed posing at the hostess stand like a medicated Disney princess waiting to seat customers and to blow up balloons for kids. Rather than stick to my job, I'd been leaving the hostess stand to help bussers clean tables, earning me respect from coworkers, who watched me blossom from a reserved, polite, young woman into a wildly extroverted, overly friendly human because eighteen-year-old me needed to interact with many people on a daily basis, manage multiple tasks at once, and most of all be of service. The manager gave in and let one of the seasoned waters train me.

To say that I loved being a waitress is an understatement. My personality expanded like one of the many balloons I'd had to blow up for Sunday brunch, my spirit rejoicing at the discovery that I was good at something other than piano or school. I liked knowing exactly when a table of four needed wet naps after a plate of ribs, and I loved being rewarded for providing good service in the form of big tips, cash that I shoved into my apron and counted in the bathroom. I felt honored whenever couples or families requested to have me as their waitress simply because I remembered their names, their food and drink choices, their kids, their birthplace, their occupation, their shoe size, which person in their family was currently in the hospital, and "Oh my God, did you get a haircut? You look so pretty."

I felt lucky to work with some of the coolest people I'd ever met, each one with a unique personality and sense of humor that endeared them to me: students, artists, optimistic entrepreneurs, single moms—all of them convinced that waiting tables was not to be a lifetime endeavor. "This is just in the meantime," they'd say as we smoked cigarettes on the loading dock behind the restaurant. "I've got plans, girl. I'm not gonna wait tables for the rest of my life, fuck that. What about you?"

Me? I had a wildly different perspective.

Having blown off a partial music scholarship to FIU, I enrolled at Miami-Dade Community College knowing I'd have to pay for my education, and I was thrilled with the opportunity to make instant cash, grateful for the flexible schedule, happy for the chance to meet so many new people and make friends outside of my high school experience. I gravitated toward Lisa, a woman ten years my senior who'd been gifted with a generous, compassionate spirit, her kind, blue eyes and genuine interest in my thoughts and perspectives a way for me to begin regarding myself as a mature young woman rather than a teenager. Lisa was apple pie American, and even though my background was *arroz con leche* Latina, not once did I ever feel that my ethnicity was something to overcome; never did I feel weird or uncomfortable in my skin, my level of comfort around her the reason I quickly accepted an invitation to her home. "Want to come over for coffee tomorrow?" I met her beautiful family: Her husband David and her three boys, Jason, Eric, and Nicholas.

Lisa had grown up in Miami and had witnessed the influx of Cubans and other groups of Latinos into all areas of the city. Rather than run from the rapidly changing demographic, she had dived headfirst into the tidal wave of immigration, had seen it as an opportunity to learn about a new culture, to experience a new language, new foods, and music. Her zest for life and curiosity about others was much like a safety blanket for me, under which I could explore freely the new person I was becoming.

Eventually, I would come to regard her as the older sister I'd never known I needed, and for all the time I worked at TGI Fridays and even beyond, Lisa reserved a place for me at the dining room table during Thanksgiving and Christmas, these holidays memorable because never did they comment on how little I ate, how many cigarettes I smoked, or how much I drank. Around Lisa and her family, I felt free, my only regret that I was too ashamed to share with Lisa just how deep I'd fallen into an eating disorder. It was difficult for me to sit down at the table without my heart racing and my hands shaking, the temptation to binge and purge so great that instead I'd drink and chain smoke to keep my mind off of it lest I purge in her bathroom and cause it to clog, *qué pena*.

There was never a dull moment at the restaurant, what with the hustle and bustle on most nights, waiters jumping to attention upon hearing the kitchen expediter screaming "I NEED FOOD RUNNERS, GOD DAMN IT!", the merciless practical jokes we played on each other, the mid-shift smoke breaks on the back loading dock, the heartfelt hugs for the Haitian grandpa who washed dishes, that one waitress who cussed a whole bunch and sassed the line cooks, "Where the fuck is my order for table twelve?", the drunk guy at the bar always falling off his stool, the woman at table forty-two complaining nonstop about the air conditioning, or the mother of two small children asking for crackers "in the meantime," a busboy immediately grabbing the broom and dustpan because the Saltines would end up all over the floor, the crazy waiter screaming, "I'm in the weeds!" and everyone coming together to help deliver drinks or salads or breadsticks, the over-worked manager sweating buckets as he took off his tie and jumped in the kitchen to lend a hand on a busy Friday night, all the chaos and stress vanishing into thin air as we put up the last chair and bar stool and walked out the door, only to hang out in the parking lot for a few beers before we all went home, bundles of cash in our pockets and smiles of relief on our faces because the Night. Was. Over.

What was there not to love?

Lisa made me feel heard and seen and loved, but I was also desperate to fit in with everyone else; I wanted to feel part of this magnificently crazy work family, so I kept my job satisfaction to myself lest I be labeled weird, instead choosing to be empathetic and validating and understanding whenever someone bitched about having to wait tables because as young as I was, people seemed ready and willing to openly share with me their frustrations and dreams, perhaps hoping I could point them in the right direction when all I could really do was pick up their Sunday brunch shift or give them a ride home.

Fun or not, working in a restaurant environment did nothing for my physical health. I was surrounded by people most of whom smoked heavily, drank often, and experimented with all manner of drugs, people to whom I gravitated simply because they were so raw, so authentic, their blessed ability to withhold judgment on my life path a safe haven for my own insecurities, men and women both young and old who thought nothing of inviting me to a party and not giving two shits about how much I drank or smoked, the same people who must have sensed that drugs would've been the end of me because they made sure nobody passed me the joint, or a line of cocaine, or placed a tiny piece of paper on my tongue that would send me on a trip to God knows where.

Drinking and smoking transitioned from habits into lifestyle, both becoming firmly ensconced in my young life because rather than feel judged, I felt welcomed. Allowed.

Accepted.

Bulimia still ruled my life, though, forever dictating the flow of my days and the stability of my moods, my willingness to attend any social engagements like a party or a date largely dependent on whether or not I'd woken up feeling skinny enough, whether or not I'd been able to see my ribs in the mirror when I sucked in my stomach, and if not, a last minute cancelation of that party or date would follow, "I'm sorry but I'm not feeling well," my anxiety through the roof until I binged and purged enough times to feel satisfied and in control again, my mood bordering on manic until I could once again see my ribs in the bedroom mirror.

Working in a restaurant was a daily reminder that food was simply inescapable, a reality I couldn't avoid. I'd walk through my station with a quick smile for anyone who caught my eye, something akin to happiness radiating from me until I caught a glimpse of someone enjoying their chicken fingers or potato skins, until I noticed a couple coming together over fried mozzarella sticks or mocha mud pie, my spirit missing all those years when I ate like everyone else, with no thought to calories, or being skinny, or where to purge. That I no longer remembered what it was like to eat with abandon saddened me, the exposure to so many people enjoying food a form of mental torture.

Yet no amount of sadness could trump the happiness I felt whenever I saw my rail thin body in a mirror. Sadness didn't stand a chance against the attention I received from the opposite sex, both at work and at school. My hair, light brown and curly, had grown down to my waist. My walks and day trips in Mexico had turned my skin the color of gold, my teeth settling nicely into my mouth and leaving me with a slight overbite that one waiter referred to as "sexy."

I loved being wanted, loved being described as sexy and beautiful, and nowhere near wanting to let that go for the sake of good health. Happiness was rooted in my appearance and how others perceived me, deeply entrenched in the warrior persona I'd chosen to adopt because I liked her so much more than the fat, insecure teenager; surely everyone else preferred her as well. Skinny was synonymous with confidence, strength, and power.

I waitressed full time and went to school, all of my previous worries and fears about the future buried under my hectic schedule, my free time spent mostly on studying or sleeping or hanging out with my new friends from work. As in Mexico, I relied heavily on coffee, Blow Pops, and sunflower seeds for sustenance, at times buying a banana nut muffin in the morning to have with my coffee, always careful to eat only a few tiny pieces off the top lest I eat too much and have to purge before class. My eating disorder was a serious problem, and I smoked and drank entirely too much, but still I believed I had everything under control.

And then I fell in love.

I'd made a promise to myself at fifteen that I would never get married or have children, but that never stopped me from wanting to fall in love, to feel what I'd read about in books or seen in movies. My high school years had been marked by a few brief relationships with boys who'd paid the price for being too nice, too easy, too predictable, my expectations for how love should feel having ruined their chances of conquering my heart. Each breakup had resulted in guilt on many levels: guilt for having broken someone's heart—"I'm so, so sorry"—guilt for having been too messed up and weird and picky, guilt for not having been like all the other normal girls whose lives revolved around their boyfriends. And whereas Papi had always been hands off, Mami's emotional entanglements with each of my boyfriends had added an extra layer of guilt, which had made feel worse for wanting to experience true love.

"*Pero* why did you break up with *el Guido*? He loves you so much, and he was so nice to you."

"I know, Mami, but I just . . . I don't know. I am not 'in love' with him, you know? *No lo amo.*"

"*Ay, mija*, I don't know what's wrong with you. You're

too picky. *Pobrecito el Guido, ay Dios mío.*"

With crazy high expectations tucked into my metaphorical suitcase, I walked into TGI Fridays, no serious relationships under my belt and my virginity intact. On my very first day of work, I ambled into the service bar area and had locked eyes with one of the bartenders, whose intense stare had quite literally taken my breath away. *Oh my God*, I thought, *love at first sight is not a rumor after all.*

I'd gone home that day, hoping the guy with the New Jersey Red Devils baseball cap would ask me out soon, but it would take a full year before he'd make any effort. He paid little attention to me after that first day, but that didn't stop me from doing research, from listening to other waitresses talk about the tall young man with the lopsided grin, light eyes, and dark wavy hair long enough to be sexy without being weird.

"He's so sexy, but I heard he has a girlfriend."

"That's too bad. He's really mysterious, don't you think?"

"He seems like such a tortured soul, but it's part of the appeal, right?"

"I wonder where he's from. Someone said he's from New Jersey."

"Well, I heard he and the girlfriend broke up. Apparently, she was cheating on him, can you believe that? I would never cheat on a guy like that."

"Yeah, that's awful. I heard his father died recently, and I think his mom died, too."

"There's something about his eyes, they're so intense and raw, like you can tell he's super deep."

I stored each tidbit of information in my heart, which seemed to want him more each day, the mystery and the darkness like powerful magnets pulling me toward him. I stared at him whenever I thought he wouldn't notice, stumbled and mumbled and babbled whenever I had to order drinks at the service bar. His intense stare repeatedly caused my face to turn crimson as I walked out of the service bar area with my tray of Gold Medalists and Long Island iced teas.

By the time he asked me out exactly one year from the day we locked eyes, I decided that he was The One, the man I would marry, this belief fully validated by the long-awaited butterflies I felt in my stomach when he cradled my face with both hands and leaned in to kiss me, gently at first but then passionately. *Oh my God,* I thought. *It's true, it's true, it's true. Love is real.* My promise to Papi that I would focus on being independent was completely forgotten as we walked hand in hand around the Miami Beach Art Festival on our first date, my heart beating so wildly that I believed I'd found my soul mate, my missing piece, my eighties movie finally playing out in real life.

Love intoxicated me, found its way into every crevice of my broken self, my fear of losing him so intense that I failed to see all the ways in which the relationship would devastate me, his traumatic past something I hadn't thought would be a problem because I'd had no idea a cheating ex and the tragic death of his parents would turn him into a possessive and controlling boyfriend, into a *novio* whose love for me justified his need to know my every move. "I just worry about you." His fear of abandonment was so real that my having dated other guys before him sparked a scary level of anger, "YOU LIED TO ME! How can I trust you! What else are you lying about?"

His capacity for trust having been destroyed, he

looked at me shortly after we had sex for the first time and snickered, "I don't believe you were a virgin," those seven words crushing my heart because I'd been saving my precious virginity for The One. Having it invalidated and dismissed was the last thing I'd ever expected, and it made me feel shameful and dirty, as though perhaps I'd made a terrible mistake.

Mami's approach to sexual matters stemmed from the Dark Ages, but I felt compelled to tell her, wondered if perhaps I'd feel better about the whole thing if she knew that my precious virginity was gone for good.

She was ironing a pair of Papi's pants when I decided to broach the subject, her tiny frame not much higher than the ironing board, a cigarette burning in an ash tray as she sang along to Vicente Fernandez' "*Lástima Que Seas Ajena.*" I wanted badly to get the truth off my chest, but seeing her with a hot appliance in her hands gave me momentary pause. I'd once seen Abuele Meche lose her shit and throw a hot iron at Tia Yolanda, and I worried perhaps Mami had inherited that same level of crazy.

"Mami," I said, "I need to ask you something."

She remained focused on ironing, pausing only to spray the pants with some water. "*Ándale, mija*, what is it?"

"Well, uh, what would you do if I told you *que* I'm no longer a virgin?"

She continued to iron, Papi's pants looking better by the second. "*Bueno, mija*, what do you want me to do, eh? Do you want me to sew you back up?"

No way did she say that, I thought, but before I could reply, she stopped ironing, grabbed the cigarette out of the ashtray, and took a drag, eyeing me with curiosity as she blew out the smoke. "*Oye, mija*, was it recent?"

"*Sí*, Mami, a few weeks ago."

"Uh-huh," she said, "*y porqué* you wait so long?" She was smiling, trying not to laugh.

I wondered if Mami was indeed losing it, if perhaps she had me confused with someone else. "Maaaaami! You told me I had to wait!"

She sighed and shook her head from side to side. "*Ay, mija*, and you believed me? I thought you'd been having sex with *el Guido* in high school, because you would come home with your lips all swollen and your hair *todo un desastre*."

"I wasn't!"

"*¿Y el Roberto?*"

"No!"

"*¿Ni Max?*"

"No!"

Mami and I crossed a border that day, our relationship exploring new territory in which conversations about having sex and even birth control were allowed, but still she maintained that my life would be complete only after I got married and had children, a belief that she'd been hinting at for years. "You'll understand when you have your own children. You'll know what I mean when you get married."

But I could no longer imagine getting married to The One, not when our relationship felt more like a never-ending emotional roller coaster, a scary ride that never stopped him from trying to convince me to elope. "I just want to take you away to live in a small town, to lock you away in a house where only I can see you, because I love you so much, and I don't want to share you."—words that at first had made me feel special and *oh so loved,* but later scared the butterflies away, the magic spell under which I'd been slowly washed away by the tears I cried each time he broke up with me for being a liar or a *traicionera.*

Our relationship bordered on manic and triggered intense episodes of bingeing and purging, the only thing that made me feel better whenever we got into an argument or whenever I felt like I'd done something to disappoint him. Any conversation about graduating from college and doing something with my life resulted in arguments that petrified me because his words would shut me down and render me speechless. "You don't care about me, you only care about yourself!" His grief and pain showed up as demons that encouraged him to engage in sporadic drug use that provoked unpredictable mood swings I tried every which way to prevent by being less friendly and less charming with my customers at work, by wearing pants instead of skirts, by refraining from wearing make-up or looking too cute, by avoiding scenarios like laughing with a fellow waiter or sneaking out for a smoke break by myself, the constant walking on eggshells exhausting me to no end and making me wonder if I'd ever find a way out. I'd grown scared of him, and I spent most of my mental energy on pacifying him, on making sure I didn't disappoint him or make him angry with me. I didn't realize at the time that his behavior was abusive.

A few weeks before my twenty-first birthday, I was sitting in Papi's armchair watching CNN, the smell of *sofrito* permeating the entire house as Mami worked her magic in the kitchen, my stomach growling and my stress level high because I had two toxic relationships in my life: one with my *novio* and one with food. Watching the news somehow brought me comfort, the images of other countries on the screen reminding me that there was another world outside of the one in which I lived.

My eyes left the screen for a moment and drifted toward one of the framed pictures hanging just above the television. It was a picture of me and my cousin Lorena, our arms around each other and smiles on our faces as we posed in front of *Teatro Degollado*, a theater in the central plaza of Guadalajara. It made me a little sad that only two years prior, while we'd driven across the southern United States on our way to Mexico, while I'd roamed the streets of Guadalajara and sat on a bus traveling down a dirt road to Tonalá, I had been a dreamer with a backpack, a wannabe vagabond, a warrior on a mission to do something different and impactful. The realization that I had buried that piece of me frustrated me because I'd once promised myself that I would live a different life, one in which no man would ever tell me what to do, where to go, how to dress, or who to talk to. This vision of me as a badass single *guerrera* thankfully provided the *ganas* I needed at that moment to walk away from my toxic relationship, my heart in pieces all the same because no matter how much he scared me, he'd been my first love, the person with whom I had imagined saying *I do*, the guy who hadn't been too nice or too predictable or too easy but instead too hurt in ways I was too young to understand, let alone heal.

After we broke up, he showed up at my house more than a few times and threw rocks at my bedroom window in the middle of the night, followed me home, and questioned where I'd been and with whom, our permanent breakup noticed by everyone at Friday's because he couldn't control himself. "Who are those guys sitting at your station? Is that your new boyfriend?" Finally, he quit his bartending job and left, his parting gift weighing on me for months: "You'll never amount to anything but a shitty waitress," his last words fueling my determination to be a *guerrera* for the rest of my life. *Fuck that.*

Papi had kept quiet throughout our tumultuous *we broke up-we're back together-we broke up again* relationship. Mami couldn't help but be who she'd always been, a woman who hated to see people suffering, "*Pobrecito,* he's so hurt." I couldn't expect her to understand my reasons for breaking up with him because in her eyes, he was "*un buen muchacho;*" after all, he'd never hit me or cheated on me, and he had proven to be hard working, "*muy trabajador,*" qualities she deemed valuable enough to justify the verbal and psychological abuse that I'd experienced, her view of relationships having come straight out of a *telenovela;* it was more important to have a man in my life than pursue a career or something as silly as my own dreams. Her firmly entrenched views clashed with mine and fueled my desire to live my own life and on my own terms, this renewed promise to be fiercely independent and unattainable the reason I would eventually push away every single guy who dared to love me.

My love for school and dreams of doing something different with my life helped me to forget about The One. I still obsessed about my weight and my appearance, but no longer did I experience racing thoughts and overwhelming emotions that triggered intense episodes of bingeing and purging. During my first two years in community college, I embraced all of the required classes my peers found boring, like Humanities and The Social

Environment. I enrolled in electives that seemed interesting: Oceanography. Human Sexuality. Intro to Philos-
ophy. Intro to Logic. I joined the college choir, grateful
that I'd found a way to keep four-part harmony in my
life, and I applied to FIU for the last two years of school.
I was a few weeks out of my relationship with The One
when I started my junior year, International Relations as
my declared major.

Once again there had been no strategy behind my
choice of major, no thought to what door it might open,
where it would take me, how much money I would make.
During my second year at Miami-Dade Community College, I'd registered for Intro to International Relations,
hoping it would be public relations on an international
level, having been told many times by customers that I
had great people skills and should "do" public relations,
whatever that meant.

I'd loved Intro to International Relations from day
one, had felt a familiar excitement when our Yugoslavi-
an professor had opened his mouth and began to discuss
the collapse of his country and the factors leading up to
its demise, the way he'd paused to share with us his own
experiences as a young man in Yugoslavia under Tito. I'd
realized quickly the class was far from public relations, but
I'd remained seated, too respectful of the professor to walk
out, and too enthralled with the subject matter anyway.

It remains one of the best mistakes I've ever made.

I hoped a degree in International Relations would
satisfy my desire to learn more about the world, prayed
it would help me better understand global conflicts and
fill the huge void left by my public-school education,
in which I was taught America was the center of the

universe, and English the only language worth a dime. The word *international* appealed to me, reminded me that I was participating in something bigger than me, gave me hope that perhaps I could get a job that involved traveling and meeting people who had different lived experiences, spoke other languages, practiced other religions.

But in reality, I couldn't conceptualize what I would do or "be" with a degree in International Relations and had little time to think about it because after two years of waitressing, I was promoted to bartender, my schedule becoming busier than ever.

In classrooms, I explored the history, economics, and politics of other countries and tried to wrap my head around theories, while bartending provided me with a first-rate education in human behavior. My good friends Johnny Walker, Jose Cuervo, and Jack Daniels were experts at getting people to talk, at shifting behavior from reserved to friendly to "I need help with my marriage." My own curiosity sparked question after question and helped me fill the tip jar with enough money to pay for each semester in cash. And even though I often made over one-hundred fifty a night, even though I could pick up a shift at the drop of a hat and put money in my pocket, bartending could not be a forever job, would never be a "real" job, not when I was working toward a Bachelor's degree and the promise of a life beyond what my parents had achieved.

Worried about what people would think, Mami was not thrilled with my promotion to bartending. "Women don't belong behind a bar, *mija*," a concern that quickly disappeared after I started slipping her cash to play bingo. Papi said nothing, instead remaining a silent force whose presence alone reminded me that his expectations for me extended beyond flipping bottles, pouring drinks, and cleaning ashtrays.

Papi and I had many conversations about my college courses, discourses during which we clashed on fundamental theories and politics because anything to the left of his perspective was socialism or communism and therefore the work of Satan. I found my voice during that time, embraced the freedom to develop and share my own perspectives with conviction, found that although I was surrounded by staunch Republican Cubans who openly criticized *los demócratas* and the socialist platform that never seemed to materialize, I leaned to the left when it came to civil rights, health care, and education, and not once did I ever feel afraid to share my thoughts with Papi.

Our debates added a valuable dimension to my education, Papi's ability to listen to my opposing views and to engage in healthy dialogue teaching me the value of respect because even though our positions at opposite ends of a spectrum could have ignited a war, Papi was curious without judgment, respectful as opposed to dismissive and rude.

He provided me with space to explore my value system and the issues that provoked in me anger or passion, the global causes about which I felt strongly: protecting the environment, eradicating poverty, putting an end to the exploitation of other countries, fighting discrimination and racism, challenging limitations on women's rights.

My views were rooted in compassion; I cared deeply for others, felt invested in their wellbeing, be it a waiter suffering from a broken heart or a busboy with a sick mother. I openly shared my concerns, always offering to listen and help, their sadness or worry finding a home in my own heart and reminding me to check in with them each time we worked together. "¿*Y tu mamá?* How is she doing?"

It was not unreasonable for me to care for others as my parents had consistently shown me that we were the kind of people who thought nothing of helping complete strangers. I have numerous memories of my father, many that make me laugh out loud, yet the ones I cherish are those in which he demonstrated genuine compassion for others, special moments that taught me how to love a fellow human being.

One such memory finds me at ten years old, my chubby, sweaty thighs sticking to the seats of our pick-up truck on a Saturday morning, a grocery list tucked safely into the small purse Papi had bought me on our last trip to Tijuana before we'd moved to Miami. It was miserably hot and humid that day, no amount of air conditioning able to save us from the blistering sun reflecting off the dashboard. I didn't mind it so much, not when I knew Papi would buy me *un batido de mamey* from the little café near the Winn-Dixie.

We were cruising along Bird Road when Papi suddenly pulled over.

I looked around, wondering what happened. "Why are we stopping, Papi?"

He turned off the engine and opened his door. "Come with me, *mija. Ven conmigo.*"

I looked around again. "For what?"

Cubans rarely use their finger to point at something or someone, opting to use their lips instead. Papi puckered his lips toward a thin, white haired man in slippers and pajamas shuffling down the sidewalk. I jumped out of the truck, pulled my T-shirt down to cover my protruding belly, and chased after Papi as he approached the *viejito*.

"Papo," he said, "where are you going?" Papi placed his hand gently on the man's arm. The old man looked at Papi, not a shred of recognition on his face as he shrugged his shoulders as though to say, "I don't know."

"Where do you live, *mi viejo?"*

The old man came to life. *"¿Yo? ¡En Cuba!* I live in Camaguey, *muchachón."*

"What do you have in your hand?" Papi asked. "Is that your wallet? May I see it?"

"Sí, joven, here." He handed the wallet to Papi. *"Mi novia* is waiting for me, *¿me oíste?* She lives in Havana, so I need to catch the next bus." Papi thankfully found an identification. *"Oye,* do you think she's still waiting for me?"

Papi smiled. *"Claro que sí, papo. Dale,* I'll take you. *Mija,* help me get him in the truck."

We buckled him in and drove the ten minutes to his home, where we met his very worried daughter and wife. They had called the police soon after realizing he'd wandered off. They were beyond grateful and offered us something to drink and eat: *"¿Quieres un cafecito? ¿Un pastelito de guayaba?"* But Papi would never accept compensation for a good deed, choosing instead to give them our phone number just in case the old man wandered off again.

I reference that day as the moment I learned to care for people I didn't know, to worry for the safety of complete strangers. It was an example of compassion that came to inform and shape my own identity as I navigated my college experience and tried to formulate a plan for my life.

Compassion helped me explore both sides of the Arab-Israeli conflict, and it shaped the way I viewed economic policies and political ideologies. I dove headfirst into the history of the United Nations, the conflict in the Middle East, and Soviet Foreign Policy in the 1950s, along the way learning theories, policies, and ideas that expanded my horizons and deepened my awareness of myself as a global citizen—all of it leading to seemingly impossible scenarios in which I was paid to travel the world and help others in need. My college professors fueled my dreams of traveling by sharing their experiences with humanitarian efforts in Haiti and Africa and Latin America, their stories providing me with a platform on which I could almost visualize a realistic future for myself.

Almost.

It was hard for me to imagine life after college, for as much as I had always loved school, initially I'd struggled to believe that I would graduate; nobody in my world had gone the distance and shown me it was possible. The only person who'd ever given me a glimpse was Daniel, my good friend from Karate, but any access to his friendship had been severed by a wildly jealous Puerto Rican girl who'd given him an ultimatum when I returned from Mexico: "Either cut ties with her or kiss me goodbye." I never spoke with or saw him again.

With no example within my own family to reference, rather than approach my future with a lens on real world examples and realistic opportunities, I allowed my dreams to extend beyond my limited capacities and understanding of the world, a world in which you needed to be related to someone who knew someone else who could connect you to someone at the top who had serious pull and could help you get your foot in the door. The connections of our family could no doubt hook me up with new tires for my car but connecting me to someone in the world of influential white people was an impossible stretch.

Naively I believed that, at twenty-two years old, I could pass the Foreign Service exam and work in an embassy because nobody had told me otherwise. I imagined working for the United Nations in who knows what capacity or for the Peace Corps. I visualized working for an overseas nonprofit organization in which I would help build a school or teach English, dreams that had nothing to do with money because I yearned for something impactful, something that had meaning and purpose, something beyond mixing cocktails and serving fried mozzarella sticks.

What little information I had regarding opportunities post college was gleaned from conversations with fellow students in my program, many of whom talked about going to law school or graduate school, neither of which appealed to me because I wanted badly to travel, to visit the countries about which I had learned so much, to experience the cultures I'd only read about, to talk to people outside of my own Cuban/Mexican world. It mattered little how much I drank or smoked or binged and purged, my unhealthy physical and mental state had no impact on my dreams. Believing I had something of value to offer the external world, I paid little attention to my broken internal world: the daily bingeing and purging, the drinking and smoking, the bags under my eyes, and the hours I spent in front of the mirror analyzing my body and searching for signs of weight gain. *Can I still see my ribs? Can I still see my hip bones?*

Abuela Meche's words haunted me, encouraged me,

"Someday you will know what this life wants from you," their implication challenging me to drop the idea that a steady income and a retirement plan were the key to happiness, a mindset that was both uncomfortable and scary because it wasn't what I'd been taught to believe about life. As much as my parents wanted me to get an education, never did they encourage me to explore jobs for the sake of happiness or fulfillment; instead, they emphasized the importance of financial stability and a good credit score, Papi constantly reminding me that I would have to make *sacrificios* sooner or later.

I kept my dreams to myself, lest I worry my parents with too much talk of leaving the nest, anxiety creeping up on me as graduation day loomed closer and closer, panic overwhelming me as I walked across a stage for the second time in my life to receive a diploma, the pride I should have felt at being the first person in my family to get a college education buried underneath the shame of having no clear life plan, and that grim reality weighing on me as I agreed to pick up a bartending shift for one of my fellow bartenders that same night, a decision that would bring me proof of God's sense of humor because *"Solo Dios sabe lo que hace."*

ONLY GOD KNOWS

FOREIGN LANGUAGES FASCINATED ME; SOMEONE SPEAK-
ing in an unfamiliar tongue sent a thrill of excitement
right through me, like a lightning bolt of expectation and
wonder. They offered me a sneak peek into another realm,
a way for me to recognize that I was in the presence of
someone who was different from me, someone to whom
I naturally gravitated in the hopes that they would teach
me something about their world. That this mild obsession would help me fulfill my dreams of traveling was not
something I had been strategizing, planning, researching,
exploring, or discussing with anyone, because I hadn't
been able to connect this curiosity to an actual profession.
Ignorant to whatever paths existed beyond the straight
one to becoming a doctor, a lawyer, a nurse, or a teacher, I'd never imagined that asking one simple question,
"Where are you from?" would change my life in the most
incredible of ways and indeed set me on a different path.

Having agreed to work the night shift for a fellow bartender, I changed out of my graduation outfit and into
my work uniform, my passion for learning more about
the world promptly replaced by a red and white striped
shirt, black suspenders, and black pants, an old familiar
question on my mind as I pulled my hair up into a tight
ponytail: *What am I going to do? What am I doing to do?
What am I going to do?*

Dreams about traveling the world had done a good
job of helping me avoid the future. I hadn't given life beyond graduation day any serious consideration, had only
flirted with applications for graduate school or law school,

neither of which had seemed like a good idea for as much as I'd loved every class within the INR program, much like my experience with piano I'd known from the beginning that INR would never be my forever gig. My approach to getting a college degree had been a pragmatic one. *If I'm paying for this degree, I may as well study something that interests me.* Rather than something I'd wanted to *do* or *be*, a degree in International Relations had been a door to another world to which I'd never been exposed.

But all that learning, exploring, theorizing, and contemplating had not been enough to dispel my anxiety about the future. Much like when I'd graduated from high school, I found myself feeling the same way only one day after college graduation: lost and afraid.

I smoked two cigarettes on the way to work, and I tried to keep my mind in the same space I'd inhabited for the last four years, one in which the future had seemed miles away, but the distance between me and *the rest of my life* shortened instantly the moment I stepped behind the bar and back onto the island of booze from which I now wanted to be rescued.

Knowing I'd just graduated, the other bartender Patty congratulated me, her smile genuine and warm. As always, I pretended to be happy and relieved, pretended that I was thrilled with my inability to have formulated a life plan.

"You must be so happy, Yvonne. What are you going to do now?" she said.

"Oh, I'm in no hurry to figure that out," I lied. "I want to enjoy not being in school for a while, save some money, and go see my family in Mexico at the end of the summer. I'm not too worried, though."

"I'm sure you have a plan, but don't get stuck behind

this bar forever, girl! I wish I'd gone to college but with two babies now, forget it." She walked away, and I went back to washing glassware. I kept my head down and scrubbed beer and wine glasses, selfishly hoping we'd have a slow night for once.

"Hey, Patty," I said a few moments later, "do you mind if I do more of the restocking and bar-backing stuff tonight? I have a lot of energy to burn off, you know what I mean?"

"Hell, yeah! I hate doing that stuff. I'll take care of customers and let you know when I need help."

I focused on keeping my hands busy by restocking beer and ice, cleaning glassware, running food—anything to keep me in motion and my mind empty of thoughts. *It's going to be okay. What am I going to do? It's going to be okay. You need to figure something out. It's going to be okay. You can't work as a bartender forever, what are people going to think? You need to get a real job, because you have a college degree. It's going to be okay. You need to get a real job. It's going to be okay. You need to get a real job. . . .*

"Excuse me, can we get some menus?" The voice was soft, a slight accent enough to get my attention. I looked up to find two men in expensive looking suits sitting in front of me, kind faces I'd never seen in the crowd of regulars we served on most nights.

"Oh, I'm sorry, I didn't see you sitting there. I'll grab you some menus." I handed them over. "Would you like something to drink?"

The older gentleman spoke again, this time with an accent that was more pronounced. "Oh yes, of course. I think I'll have a vodka tonic."

The other gentleman ordered a draft beer, my ears

straining to hear an accent and hearing none. I brought their drinks over and smiled as I waited to take their order.

The older man picked up his drink and took a sip. "Is this bar always this quiet? We have never been here before."

"It's kinda quiet during the week, especially on Mondays, but on Fridays it's pretty much a circus."

He nodded. "Ah, that makes sense."

"My name is Yvonne, by the way."

"Nice to meet you, Yvonne. I'm Werner, and this here is Victor."

I shook their hands. "Nice to meet you. So where are you from?"

Werner raised his eyebrows. "What do you mean? Like, where do we live? Or where were we born?"

"Well, I noticed you have an accent and—"

"Oh, I see what you mean. Well, let's see," he said, "before coming to Miami I lived in Hawaii, and before that I lived in California and Mexico and France. But I am originally from Austria."

Victor laughed. "I'm afraid my life has not been that glamorous. I've lived in different places, but I'm originally from Albany, New York."

Werner was staring at me intently, making me wonder if I'd offended him. "Why do you ask?"

My face turned bright red. "Because I can't help it! I'm so nosy it's embarrassing. I'm always asking people where they're from because I like learning about other countries and cultures. I hope I didn't offend you by commenting on your accent. That wasn't my intention."

Werner smiled. "Not at all, not at all. Are you in school?"

"No. I literally just graduated. Like, today. Like, a few hours ago." I laughed.

"That's wonderful! Congratulations!" He took another sip of his drink and glanced down at the menu. "What appetizer would you recommend?"

"Depends on what you're in the mood for. If you want something to put you into a food coma, get the loaded potato skins or the mozzarella sticks. If you want something less heavy, I'd go with the pot stickers. Stay away from the loaded nachos unless you're okay with being constipated for a few days."

Working in the service industry had done more than just helped me pay for school, it helped me develop a sense of humor and a boldness that helped me manage all kinds of scenarios with grace and personality, my sharp wit masking the unbearable anxiety that threatened to own me. Werner and Victor laughed openly at my suggestions.

Werner closed his menu. "You are quite convincing. We'll go with the pot stickers."

"You got it." I turned around and placed the order, feeling their eyes on me as I set up placemats, napkins, and appetizer plates in front of them.

"So," Victor asked, "what are you going to do now?"

There it was, the million-dollar question for which I never seemed to have the right answer, at least not one to impress them and the millions of people sitting in the invisible audience in my head. A part of me wanted to lie, to say something ridiculous like "I'm going to law school" or "I'm going to graduate school," but on that night, as I stood behind the bar that had become my second home, my hopes and dreams for the future on life support, I searched for the right words and landed on the truth, the idea of lying so depressing that the truth for once seemed like a better option, the reality that I'd never see them again making it that much easier to admit.

I fidgeted when I was nervous, so I grabbed a bar towel and mindlessly picked up a bottle of vodka and began to wipe it down. "What am I going to do now? That's a great question. Do you want me to give you the right answer or the real answer?" I put the bottle down and picked up a bottle of rum, wiping it down slowly.

Victor laughed. "I have a feeling the right answer will be boring, so give us the real answer."

"Deal. The truth is I don't know what I'm going to do. I am still trying to figure that out."

"What did you study in college? What was your degree?" Werner asked.

"International Relations."

"Ah, that's an interesting degree. Why did you pick that major?"

"Another great question." I put down the bottle of rum and picked up the bottle of gin. "Well, knowing that I had to pay for my education, I couldn't imagine studying something like business or marketing. I didn't want to waste my money and time on something that would bore me to death." I put down the bottle of rum. "International Relations seemed interesting to me, so I went with that."

Victor raised his eyebrows and shared a glance with Werner. "You put yourself through school?"

"I sure did."

"Now *that* is refreshing," Werner said. "You must be very proud of yourself."

"I am, but I'm also super tired! Don't get me wrong- I'm glad I didn't have to take out student loans, but I've been in school full time and working full time for the past four years, and I'm probably sleep deprived."

Werner laughed. "I bet! You deserve a break." He took a sip of his drink. "What did you like about International Relations?"

"Learning about the rest of the world. I've been living in Miami for most of my life, and other than Mexico, I've never been anywhere. And now that I've learned so much about other parts of the world, the last thing I want to do is settle into a nine to five job I'll probably hate or sit in a classroom for another two or three years."

"What do you want to do?"

I paused, wondering how ridiculous my impossible dream would sound once I said it out loud. *Just tell the truth,* I thought. *You have nothing to lose.* "Honestly? I just want to travel."

Werner cocked his head to one side. "Really? And to where?"

"That's a tough question because the world is so big! Tajikistan, India, Israel, the Ivory Coast, Morocco, Croatia, South Africa, Colombia, Argentina, Zimbabwe, Jordan, never mind all the countries in Europe: Italy and France and Spain and England."

"Wow," Victor said, "sounds like you've given this a lot of thought."

"That's *all* I've done," I said. "I've spent the last two years dreaming about traveling, but I have absolutely no idea how to make it happen."

Victor laughed out loud. "Your honesty is refreshing."

"I'm glad you think so. Would you like another drink?"

"Sure, another drink would be great."

Werner pushed his empty glass toward me. "Make

that two."

Werner and Victor continued to ask me questions, all of which I answered truthfully and unapologetically because these two men, one from Austria and one from New Jersey, had shown me kindness and respect in a setting that often found me dodging inappropriate comments and behavior. Having always been the person to ask questions, it was refreshing to share my thoughts with two complete strangers.

"Tell me more about your family."

"Where are your parents from?"

"How long have you lived in Miami?"

"How did you like Mexico?"

"Why do you like working with people?"

"Do you speak any other language besides Spanish and English?"

We talked about religion and politics and music and sports, about my father's journey from Cuba, and Abuela Meche's resilience, about Mami's obsession with bingo, and my compassion for fellow humans. We talked about everything that mattered to me, the truth spilling out of me in a way I hadn't experienced in a long time.

I stepped away to restock beer and ice and wash glassware for Patty, and then I left the bar for a moment to check on a food order. When I returned, Werner signaled for the check.

"Here you go," I said, moving their empty glasses off the bar and wiping it down. Werner pulled out his wallet and placed an American Express credit card on top of the bill. "I'll take that for you, just give me a second." When I brought it back for him to sign, he was holding a business card in his hand.

"Yvonne, it has been such a pleasure to meet you. Victor and I were just talking about how much we enjoyed this conversation."

"Oh, thank you! The pleasure was all mine."

"We liked you so much that Victor and I think you should come and work with us."

Shit, I thought. *Please don't tell me you own a strip joint or something creepy like that.* "Oh, wow, thank you. But, um, now that I think about it, you never told me what you do for a living."

"Take the card," Victor said. "It should answer your question."

Trying hard to play it cool, I took the card and looked at it, not sure what to expect and worried that I'd be grossly disappointed.

Werner Neuteufel
Senior Vice President, Hotel Operations
Norwegian Cruise Lines

I sensed the ground underneath my feet shifting, my universe turning upside down as I worked on keeping my voice steady. "Cruise lines . . . wait, what does this mean?"

Werner got up from the barstool, making to leave when suddenly I wanted to ask him a million questions. "It means we'd like for you to work on one of our cruise ships. You want to travel, right?"

I lost my breath in that moment and tried to string a sentence together without sounding like an idiot. "Yes, of course I do."

"Well, call that number tomorrow and speak to my assistant. I will let her know that you might be calling. The SS *Norway* is in port on Saturday, and we're thinking it would be a good idea to invite you onto the ship to have lunch with the captain and get a tour. How does that sound?"

"Are you kidding me?" I wanted to scream.

They might have thought I was playing it cool, but in reality, I was too stunned to react appropriately, too shocked to jump up and down and give them both a bear hug, too overwhelmed to scream at the top of my lungs with joy and run around the restaurant kissing every single person.

"Sounds good," I said, my heart beating wildly. "I'll call this number first thing tomorrow morning."

"Excellent, Yvonne. You have a good night." Werner winked at me before walking away with Victor.

I ran to the bathroom with Werner's business card in my hand, overwhelmed with emotions I simply didn't know how to process because nothing remotely similar had ever happened to me. Rather than share the news with anyone, I sat alone in the tiny staff bathroom that reeked of cigarettes, wanting to cherish the moment in which I finally understood what Abuela Meche meant when she said, *"Solo Dios sabe lo que hace."*

Only God knows His plans.

A few days after touring the SS *Norway*, I met with the Human Resources Director, an older woman who seemed not at all pleased by how I'd gotten the opportunity, going so far as to insinuate that I'd slept my way into the job, an assumption about which I did nothing because I was too afraid to mess up the opportunity. Toni was in charge of my paperwork, my ship assignment, my life for the next six months and beyond. I asked a few questions that she answered impatiently, her last words to me a reminder to refrain from sharing with anyone how I'd gotten the job. "We get thousands of applications each week, you know. Not everyone gets chosen this way." Getting a job on a cruise ship was no small feat, a factor that made me feel even more special as I drove home in utter disbelief at how quickly my life had changed, Van Morrison's "Into the Mystic" at full volume as I headed west on the Dolphin Expressway, thinking *Thank you, God. Thank you, God. Thank you, God.* I gave no thought to how Mami and Papi would react until I pulled up in front of the house. At no point in time had I considered what they would think or whether they'd approve, but as much as Papi encouraged me to be independent and strong, I still needed and wanted their approval of whatever I did. Mami had helped me pick out what to wear that morning, offering encouragement as she set up the ironing board and grabbed the dress out of my hands. "*Ándale, mija,* take a shower or you're going to be late."

When I walked in the door, I found her in the kitchen making dinner and Papi in his favorite armchair, *Noticias Telemundo* on the television filling the house with the current horrors taking place all over the world; floods, landslides, earthquakes, *chupa cabra* sightings, kidnappings, bombings, children murdered, women raped, men gathered and tortured by a guerilla group—whatever news would give viewers something to discuss with friends and family, something to make them feel more fortunate. "*Ay Dios mío,* did you see what happened in Guatemala? Did you hear about that woman who was murdered by her sister's husband? Did you hear what happened to Juanita?"

"*¡Hola!*" I said, unable to hide my happiness and excitement.

Papi turned down the volume, and Mami stopped what she was doing, as though sensing I had big news to share.

"*Bueno, ¿y qué?*" Papi asked. "How did it go?"

"I got the job, Papi! I start this Friday."

"*¿Tan pronto?*" Mami asked, as she lit up a cigarette. "That's fast, *mija*, they must have loved you. *Entonces, ¿cómo es?* What's the job and where is it?"

Her eyes held so much expectation. So much love. So much faith in me. So much of everything making it hard to deliver the news that I would be leaving home for at least six months.

"Um, *bueno*, it's a job *en un crucero,* on a cruise ship," I said.

Papi got up from the armchair and sat at the kitchen counter. He lit up a cigarette as though ready to launch into a discussion about the rise of Islamic Fundamentalism. "*Espérate, ¿cómo es eso?*" he said. "*Cómo que* it's on a cruise ship? What does that mean?"

"Well, it's a job where I work on the ship as a purser."

"*Un purser?*" Mami asked. "What is a purser?

In truth, I knew very little, having been so eager to get the job I hadn't asked many questions for fear the opportunity would've been rescinded. "I don't know, Mami, but I think it has something to do with customer service, with helping people."

This was apparently enough for Mami, because she nodded and said, "Oh, I see, I see. That's good, *mija,* you're good with people."

Papi paused to sip the *cafecito* that had materialized out of nowhere, like a Cuban magic trick. "*Y ven acá*, are you going to work Monday through Friday?"

I avoided eye contact. "*Bueno*, um, *lo que pasa es que*, the thing is that I'm going to live on the ship. *O sea*, I stay on the ship *todo el tiempo*, for I think six months or something, but then I get to come home for two months."

Silence. Mami and Papi chewed on that last bit of information as they would an old pork rind; they wanted it to taste good, but something was off.

Papi and Mami shared a look, an understanding that although this piece of news was somewhat devastating, they would not stand in the way of this opportunity. Through marital osmosis, they put aside their sadness and instead focused on asking me questions about the size of the ship, the ports of call, what my cabin would look like, Papi of course reminding me to appreciate the opportunity and do right by those nice men who'd hand-picked me from a bar at TGI Fridays, whatever sadness he may have felt trumped by the smile on my face and the promise of my future, his sacrifices and hard work coming to fruition, whatever mental and emotional battles I faced long hidden from them, put away for safekeeping until I'd find myself face to face with them, their patience with me having run out.

DRIFTING AWAY

Raz and I were jumping up and down on Mami and Papi's queen size bed, our smiles bigger than our faces, and our innocence tricking us into thinking the sound of the headboard smacking the wall wouldn't get Mami's attention. We were in sync, our feet landing on the bed at the same time until we got off sync, our uneven jumps causing the bedframe to smack even harder against the wall, *thump thump thump*, the enormous wooden crucifix above the bed making its way toward the end of the nail on which it hung and then falling off, hitting the bedframe and snapping into pieces, Jesus' head landing on the floor and rolling underneath the bed, fear consuming me as Raz opened his mouth and screamed, "Maaaaaami! She broke Jesus! Yvonne broke Jesus!"

I jumped off and crouched low to the ground, searching for Jesus' head lost somewhere in the chaos of shoes, boxes, and old toys living underneath the bed. My hand closed around it as I stood to face what I thought would be the wrath of Hilda Castañeda. Tears were already running down my face when I looked up at Mami, my four-year-old soul convinced that I would never again do anything as criminal as breaking Jesus.

"I'm sorry, Mami," I cried, "*perdóname*."

But Mami was not mad. She spent the next few hours trying to calm me down while Raz looked on, annoyed I hadn't gotten in trouble, Mami's soothing voice reminding me that I did not cause Jesus any pain. "*No, mi amor*, He suffered way before you were born. *No te preocupes, mija*, don't cry." But all the same I worried about what I'd done, this fear of hurting Jesus and going to hell so real that I begged Mami to let me glue His head back on.

And rather than alleviate this fear, my early years at St. Anthony's Catholic School in San Gabriel Valley only reinforced it. We attended St. Anthony's for a year and a half before moving to Miami, during which time I never learned the difference between right and wrong because to Sister Nancy, my first-grade teacher, *everything* we did was wrong.

Terrified of being labeled a sinner, I had slammed the heavy wooden door of the bathroom on my finger and, rather than approach Sister Nancy, I had walked back to my desk in excruciating pain and proceeded to cry, the little boy sitting next to me raising his hand to say, "Sister Nancy, Yvonne's finger is really big and blue, and it's ugly, and she's crying."

And at that moment, instead of consoling me and sending me to the school nurse, Sister Nancy had peered down her long, skinny nose at my swollen finger, a sinister smile on her face as she scolded me for slamming the door, and for needing the bathroom, and for having a weak bladder, and for drinking too much Kool-Aid. "You must pray for these sins, Yvonne." Both my finger and my heart were broken and hurting until Mami turned up and showed Sister Nancy a different version of herself, one that she hadn't learned from reading the bible or praying to Jesus, Sister Nancy's eyes growing wider by the second as Mami yelled at her because she was *straight up no kidding* super pissed off. "*Válgame Dios*, did you even look at her finger? What's wrong with you, lady?"

And yet Mami continued to believe we needed Catholicism in our lives because she enrolled us in CCD classes at St. Timothy not long after we moved to Miami, these Tuesday afternoon classes supplemented by mass every Sunday, including Palm Sunday, Easter, and Christmas, Mami's strict adherence to *la iglesia* so intense that even Papi went along with it for the sake of keeping the peace.

As a child, I didn't give much thought to whether I agreed with the teachings. I learned to say the Our Father, and Hail Mary, and the Apostle's Creed, and I was okay with the itchy, hideous, and uncomfortable white dress I had to wear for my First Communion, the celebration meal at Sizzler Steakhouse enough to make the experience worth it. I participated in the annual Christmas and Easter plays, confessed my sins to the priest who always smelled of Old Spice, and by the time Confirmation rolled around, I was a bona-fide Catholic who sang and prayed and knelt and stood and knelt and stood each and every Sunday.

Naively I believed we would keep going to church even after I was confirmed, what with Mami's crazy obsession with our attendance and our appearance. "Take off that hideous sweatshirt, *mija!* Put on a dress, and brush your hair, *¿qué van a pensar?*" The abrupt end to our Sunday routine hit me hard because as an adolescent with spiraling emotions, I had come to find solace and comfort in the smell of burning incense, in the stations of the cross, in the taste of the sacramental bread as it melted onto my tongue, in the beams of sunlight streaming through the windows high above the altar, and in the idea that, so long as I was following the rules of the church, I was doing good by Jesus and His Team.

The end of our routine made me question everything my mom had been teaching me:

"Don't lie."

"Don't do drugs."

"Don't kiss a boy with your tongue."

"Don't gossip."

"Don't tell anyone your problems."

"Don't have sex before marriage."

"Be a good student."

"Be a good girl."

"Be a good human."

But really it should not have surprised me, for as much as I'd come to cherish those Sunday afternoons, I had not been blind to the hypocritical nature of the adults in the congregation, the well-dressed, wealthy Cuban ladies who looked at Mami from head to toe and offered what could only be described as a fake-ass smile, the way Mami's behavior seemed to change around these ladies: "*Mija,* how do I look? Does my hair look okay?" And I noticed how Papi's eyes would roll back into his head whenever Mami openly commented on what she'd noticed on the drive home, all manner of judgments being thrown around. "Did you see how so-and-so looked at us? She probably thinks she's better than us. She probably gets out of the shower to pee. She's probably unhappy. I heard the *esposo* was cheating on her—all of her assumptions and judgements not going unnoticed by my fourteen-year-old self.

I wasn't okay with the end of our church routine because along the way I'd found something of value, had come to feel something that transcended the fear of sinning, something that made me feel less alone, and I held on to that "something" long after Mami put an end to our Sunday ritual.

I'd borrow Mami's Gran Prix and drive to church

on more Sundays than not, Mami and Papi heading instead to Gullermina's house in Hialeah for an afternoon of domino playing and the interminable discussion about Cuba. These solitary afternoons became my new routine, a sense of calm my only company as I drove around the city each week after mass, curiosity and sometimes boredom leading me to drive around expensive neighborhoods like Coral Gables, Coco Plum, and Coconut Grove, afternoon drives during which I thought not about the sermon but about someday living in a perfect neighborhood, with a perfect home, with a perfect lawn, with a perfect life, this yearning for perfection weighing heavily on me as I binged and purged my way through the last year of high school, the guilt I felt about what I was doing so strong that I stopped going to church, my faith overpowered by the shame of what I had become, and my relationship with God essentially broken by the time I parked my own car in front of St. Jude's Catholic Church on Brickell Avenue. It was a Monday afternoon, a few weeks into my senior year at FIU.

I'd pulled over quickly after having driven past the small church, its Romanesque Gothic style so unique to Miami that it momentarily took my breath away. *What kind of church is this?* I'd thought, its beauty eclipsing the luxury high rises all along the tree shaded avenue just off Biscayne Bay and standing out in such a way that I felt compelled to park and peek inside.

The heavy wooden door opened easily, and I stepped inside. I stood for a few moments, taking it in: the smell of aromatic incense, the stations of the cross, the holy water in which I dipped my fingers and used to bless myself, the sight of Jesus on a huge cross above the altar filling me with emotion because I suddenly felt naked and ashamed and afraid, like perhaps the years of hurting my physical body had severed whatever ties I'd had with all things Jesus and God.

And still I took a few steps forward and sat down in one of the pews, my knees finding a hassock, my eyes closing and hands coming together as the words I'd memorized so long before came back, "Our Father, who art in heaven, hallowed be—"

"Hello."

Startled, I opened my eyes and turned toward the voice. A young man dressed in clerical clothing was gazing at me, not unkindly. I sat back. "Hi," I said. "I'm sorry, um, the door was unlocked, and I assumed the church was open."

"No need to apologize," he said. "May I sit down next to you?" I nodded. He sat down, crossed his legs, and turned slightly toward me, his right arm draped across the wooden pew. "What is your name?"

"Yvonne."

"My name is Father Gabriel. It's nice to meet you."

"Nice to meet you. I take it you work here?"

He laughed. "Yes, I work here. And you? Are you a member of our church? I don't believe I've seen you here before."

"No, I'm not a member. I actually don't go to a church. I mean, I used to, like, a long time ago. I was raised Catholic."

"I see. What brought you to St. Jude on a Monday afternoon, if you don't mind my asking?"

"Well, um . . ."

I was embarrassed by the truth but couldn't imagine

lying to a priest.

". . . to be honest, I just like the way it looks from the outside. It's so different, so beautiful, like something I'd expect to see in Europe. I wanted to see the inside." I met his eyes for a moment, a sudden desire to cry overwhelming me. "I hope that's a good enough reason for Jesus." Humor was how I'd learned to mask my feelings, and it had always worked well for me, especially with strangers, but Father Gabriel was not like any other stranger I'd met. I could feel my heart racing in my chest, like maybe he was seeing right through my sense of humor.

He laughed and then grew quiet. "God doesn't much care for what brings you to Him, Yvonne. He cares more about whether or not you stay."

And with that, I unraveled, my sense of humor brushed aside by the thoughts and fears and worries that had been waiting in the wings for too long, their presence manifesting as large, endless tears that slid down my face, Father Gabriel gently placing his right arm on my back to comfort me, while the reality that I had food and shelter and safety and love made me cry even harder, because clearly I didn't know how to be grateful, didn't know how to convince myself that what I had was enough.

That I was enough.

Father Gabriel handed me a pack of tissues, and I used them to wipe my eyes and blow my nose until eventually, I stopped crying altogether. He had said nothing to me, had refrained from offering advice or from asking questions, his words as he walked me to my car hitting me with ferocious intensity, "Come back on Sunday. We'll be waiting for you." The sincerity with which he made the suggestion was enough to get me out of bed that following Sunday.

I became a member of the congregation, one of the few Latinos in a congregation consisting mostly of Lebanese, Palestinian, Syrian, and Jordanian members. St. Jude's was Melkite Catholic, an Eastern Orthodox tradition in which the mass was simultaneously conducted in both English and Arabic, my inability to understand most of what was said not enough to turn me away, because I loved the way the Arabic language landed on me, the ethereal quality of the music and songs sang *a cappella* transporting me to the Middle East and fueling my desire to see other parts of the world. And wouldn't you know it, I, too, became a member of the choir and sang in Arabic, at times stumbling to learn the songs only by ear rather than by sheet music.

Father Gabriel became a confidante, a friend, someone around whom I felt loved, but even so I refrained from sharing with him my deepest fears, my stubborn refusal to accept my imperfections and weaknesses getting in the way of any true spiritual growth. My promise to Papi that I would be strong and independent still weighed on me, my attendance each Sunday that final year of college therefore not enough to silence my fears, my weekly offerings to the church not enough to stop me from bingeing and purging each and every time I felt out of control or depressed or anxious.

But still, there was an awareness of "something" I'd felt so many years before, a connection I could not define and rather than dismiss it, I'd leaned into it as I sat on the bedroom floor the day before my college graduation, my back against the bed and my face in my hands, my silent pleas to God rooted in a request for clarity and direction, *Please, God. Please, God. Please, God. Please, God*—this

plea coursing through me as I smiled at the two gentleman who walked into TGI Friday's on a Monday night
and sat at the bar, a plea answered as Werner handed me
his business card, all my doubts lifted as I called his assistant the next morning and agreed to meet him on Saturday morning at the Port of Miami; my fears and worries
then replaced by hopeful anticipation as I toured the SS
Norway with Werner and the captain, crew members staring at me like maybe I was someone important. For the
first time in years, I had felt important and special and
chosen and lucky all at once, these feelings amplified as
I sailed away from Miami less than a week later on the
MS *Seaward*, Father Gabriel's address on a sheet of paper
tucked into my wallet. "Please keep in touch, Yvonne, and
may God bless you." I thought of Father Gabriel as the
ship made its way into the Atlantic Ocean, my struggles
with bingeing and purging and smoking and drinking
nowhere near the forefront of my mind because I hadn't
asked God to heal me, only to guide me, and maybe that
was my mistake.

TRAUMATIZED TOOTH FAIRY

I SAILED AWAY FROM MIAMI WITH A SUITCASE PACKED full of clothes, Blow Pops, and sunflower seeds, the many tidbits of advice that Mami had shared with me throughout my young life having made their way into the metaphorical suitcase in my mind, advice that she had shared with absolute conviction because she'd heard it from Abuela Meche, who'd heard it from her mother, who'd heard it from someone who had it on good authority that all of it was based on real events and therefore The Truth.

"Don't ever put your purse on the floor, *mija. Se te va el dinero*. You will lose all of your money."

"Don't leave the house with your hair soaking wet; you will catch pneumonia and die."

"Don't walk around the house barefoot—*ese frío* will cause really bad cramps."

"*Por el amor de Dios*, don't shower after you eat! You'll get a stomach cramp and fall in the shower and crack your head wide open."

Sometimes I would try to reason with her. "Mami, please. *Mira*, I'll leave the door open while I shower just in case, okay?" Other times, when I was grumpy or irritable, I'd accuse her of being superstitious and argue back. "Mami, that's ridiculous! My money is not going to vanish if I put my purse on the floor because it's in a bank account!" But her belief that my teeth would fall out unless I brushed them every day was one that I dared not question, her approach to dental hygiene a product of an unfortunate experience early on in her life.

On the morning after her wedding day, Mami had

woken up with a sense of peace, of safety, never imagining she would walk into her new bathroom and realize her peace and safety had come with a set of shiny dentures sitting in a glass of water. Apparently, her knight in shining armor had missed out on good dental care in Cuba, and this unfortunate fact coupled with a job at Sue Bee's Candies shortly after arriving in the United States meant Papi's teeth had fallen out one by one, his meager wages barely enough for dentures. This shocking revelation only one day after saying "I do" was possibly the reason she became militant in her approach to our own dental care as soon as we were old enough to hold a toothbrush. Her five-foot frame towered over us in the bathroom each and every night to make sure that we brushed our teeth vigorously. "*A ver, abre la boca,*" her eyes full of concern as she peered inside our tiny mouths to inspect our work before she followed us to our tiny bedroom, concern still on her beautiful face as she tucked us in and blessed us with the sign of the cross, no doubt praying to Jesus that our teeth escape the same fate as Papi's molars and incisors.

But her prayers were not enough to save all of my teeth, the years of bingeing and purging coupled with highly sweetened coffee and Blow Pops and whatever sugar-laden food I'd deemed safe coming together to weaken the foundation in my mouth and resulting in one of the worst maladies I'd ever suffered in my young life: a horrifying, stay up all night, *someone shoot me* kind of toothache.

I was home after my first contract on the MS *Seaward*, tan from head to toe and bubbling with stories about my coworkers; my Canadian cabin mate and English boyfriend, the Philippine crew members who worked in laundry, their smiles so genuine and warm that I couldn't help but join them on nights when they sat in the tiny hallway outside my cabin, everyone singing along whenever Benji played "Hotel California" or "Let It Be." There was the cruise staff member who spoke eight languages, the chief purser from Wales who introduced me to a whole new level of sass, the Norwegian firefighter who winked at me each and every time we crossed paths, and the nice young man from Indonesia who worked in the officer's mess. I relayed stories about my job as a member of the reception desk team, Werner and Victor having suggested to HR that I work directly with passengers. I showed them pictures of me in Cancun, me in Cozumel, me in Key West, me in Nassau, me in Norwegian Cruise Lines' private island, places that were not too far from Miami, but far enough that I'd felt glamourous and worldly.

Beyond thrilled and grateful for the new adventure, I had been excited to share a cabin the size of my bathroom at home, motivated to work seven days a week and happy to wear itchy pantyhose and super uncomfortable shoes, my smile radiant as I answered ridiculous questions like,

"What time is the midnight buffet?"

"Do these stairs go up?"

"Where do you keep the horses for the horse racing?"

"Where's the elevator that goes around the ship?"

This new experience was compounded by crew members from all over the world who came together every night in the crew bar to drink and talk and laugh and share stories, men and women of all shapes and sizes and colors and cultures who worked side by side, their conversations transcending borders and prejudice and racism, our tight quarters bringing us closer together rather than pulling us apart. Once again, I was happy to find that drinking and smoking to excess was normalized and necessary for social engagement, the idea that I'd missed out on the *going away to college experience* gone from my mind as I partied my ass off each and every night and got to know the people with whom I shared space. "Where are you from?" That I binged and purged on a regular basis was nobody's concern; I'd become a master at hiding my eating disorder.

My first contract had come to an end and with it my brief tenure with Norwegian Cruise Lines, as once again I'd found myself in the right place at the right time and with the right amount of wit and charm. On the last day of a four-day cruise, a young man from Australia had been observing me as I helped passengers from France and Brazil and Italy and Mexico understand their hefty bar and hotel charges, my proficiency in each language enough to trick said man into thinking that I would be a valuable crewmember for the new flagship of England, the MV *Oriana*, a ship for which he'd been recruiting a photography team. "I don't even know how to use a camera," I'd said, but he laughed and shrugged his shoulders. "No worries, we can teach you." I'd walked off the MS *Seaward* at the end of my contract with a literal spring in my step, happy that I'd be traveling even further away and relieved to be out of uncomfortable pantyhose and shoes that killed my feet.

Papi and Mami's patience for my endless ramblings never seemed to wane, Mami pausing to ask me how far England would be from Miami, and Papi looking at her as though to say, "*Eso no importa.*"

Only a few days before I was set to fly out of Miami for England, I was woken up with the kind of pain that I've come to regard as a broken leg and menstrual cramps combined. "Mami, I think I am dying," I'd said, this toothache so beyond painful that no amount of Orajel or Johnny Walker Black could fix it. I made an appointment with a local dentist, Dr. McDonald, breaking with the Cuban tradition of getting hooked up through a friend who has a brother who's married to the daughter of a dentist from Cuba illegally practicing out of his duplex in Hialeah and charging half the price.

"I'm sorry, Yvonne, but I'm going to have to pull it," he said, only a few moments after poking at the tooth and scoping out the rest of my mouth.

My heart dropped into my stomach. "What? Why?"

He looked somewhat pained, concerned even. "Well, um, there's really nothing I can do to save it. The decay is too great, and I wouldn't feel comfortable doing a root canal or a crown. You can always get a bridge, if you like."

Five years of bingeing and purging came crashing down on me, suffocating me and causing my palms to sweat and my throat to constrict as I admonished myself, *Don't cry. Don't cry. Don't cry. Be strong.* "Oh." I swallowed, hoping the desire to cry would pass.

He cleared his throat. "Yvonne, is there something I can do to help you?"

One look at my teeth, and he'd known, his concern boring a hole into me, the knowledge that my disease was so obviously tearing through my mouth enough to shut me down, rendering me too embarrassed and ashamed to speak, my face growing hot and beads of sweat forming across my upper lip, because there was nothing I could do to deny it, to pretend it didn't exist, to imagine that I was healthy and normal, to continue tricking myself into thinking that it would never catch up to me, that it would never pin me up against the wall and say, "It's time for a reckoning."

"No," I said, "you can go ahead and pull it." My shame went so deep that I went numb long before he injected Novocain into the surrounding gums.

When I got home, I told Papi, who reacted in the most expected of ways, with indifference and kindness all at once—"*Mija, todo tiene solución.*" But never did I imagine that losing a tooth would be a solution to anything, so I went to my room and once again, sat on the floor, my back against the bed as I allowed myself to cry and grieve a stupid, miserable tooth, my pleas to God now focusing not so much on guidance for the rest of my life but on inner strength.

Please, God. Please, God. Please, God. God, help me. Please, God, give me strength, give me strength, give me strength, my prayers rooted in a request for strength rather than a solution because I'd screwed up way too much to deserve having God resolve it for me, *así de fácil*. I cried myself to sleep that night, my pleas for strength having turned into a plea to myself, *Please change*.

Only I didn't really know what to change other than my eating habits, and although *stop throwing up* seemed like a logical solution, it was not that simple. I binged and purged not just for the sake of being skinny; it was my natural go-to whenever I felt stressed or anxious, when my pants felt a little tighter or when I felt in any way *not in control*. It was hard for me to imagine a life without this tool, impossible for me to believe that I could someday eat a whole cheeseburger and French fries without feeling immediately overwhelmed with fear and guilt.

I'd always known it wasn't a normal way to live, and whereas the fear of dying should have motivated me to change my ways, plain old vanity is what ultimately saved me, the fear of losing all my teeth and winding up with dentures enough for me to consider a whole new approach to life and to pray to God for strength.

Boarding the flight to England a few days later, I had no idea in what way strength would manifest. Would I hesitate before eating six slices of pizza and two slices of chocolate cake? Would I ignore the racing thoughts, the heart palpitations, and the fear of being fat? Would I simply walk away from the bathroom? In between drinking shandies in the morning to quickly recover from a night of heavy drinking in the crew bar of the MV *Oriana*, I kept praying for strength and tried hard to ignore the smooth skin I felt whenever I ran my tongue over the hole in my mouth, the shame and horror of having lost a tooth still weighing heavy on me.

But rather than manifest as the will to refrain from certain behaviors, strength showed up as a thought that persisted each day, as a vision of me not as a sick and unhealthy young woman but as an athlete, the image so *out of nowhere* that I began to question it, to doubt my sanity. Nobody in my immediate environment was anywhere near healthy; I was part of a team of photographers all of whom were English and Scottish, wonderful young men and women determined to drink Europe's supply of alcohol and beer, nobody ever having the bright idea to go for a run or visit the crew gym.

The vision persisted. I asked one of the ship's officers if there might be a gym for the crew members, his eyebrows raised as he pointed me in the right direction, the small room hilariously located not far from the crew bar. I took a peek and realized the only piece of equipment on which I felt moderately safe was a brand-new tread-mill. Not knowing how to lift weights or use any of the other machines, I hit START and stepped onto the belt, my improper footwear, ratty T-shirt, and old sweatpants probably not the best outfit for exercising, but I didn't care, my obsession with always looking perfect thrown out the window because I was hoping for redemption, not recognition.

I'd played soccer my senior year in high school, a tru-ly embarrassing display of athleticism because I hadn't grown up on a soccer field and knew little about the sport, having joined only because it had seemed like a good way to get exercise. But running had not been my forte, Coach Menendez screaming at the top of his lungs as I tried to get from one end of the field to the other: "Castañeda, you suck! You can't run to save your life!" And yet I found myself on a treadmill in a tiny gym on a huge ship on the Mediterranean Ocean doing just that, running to save my life.

But clearly, I was delusional. Stupidly, I'd thought that perhaps those years of Karate and that one season of soccer and those random bike rides during college would have been enough to keep me in some kind of shape, completely ignoring the hundreds and possibly thou-sands of cigarettes I'd smoked coupled with the gallons of beer and scotch and tequila, sunflower seeds, Blow Pops, and coffee having been my diet for years. I assumed I'd be able to run for at least fifteen minutes, an assumption that quite nearly killed me because after two minutes of very slow jogging, my lungs and my legs went on strike, leaving me breathless and short of collapsing, a reality that both saddened and scared me. My teeth were falling out, *and* I was grossly out of shape. *It's time for a reckoning.* I stayed on the treadmill and walked slowly for the remaining minutes, the steady pace reminding me of my childhood walks with Mami and Papi, of happier times when my only concerns were whether we'd go to Crandon Park Beach on Sunday with my whole family, whether Mami would take me to the movies to see *Breakin': Ain't No Stopping Us,* and whether Raz would let me have the last chocolate donut.

Yet I persisted, anger and frustration motivating me to visit the gym every single day. Two minutes turned into four minutes into fifteen into one mile into two miles into "Oh my God, I ran four miles," into "Hey guys, I'm going to pass on the crew bar tonight." This newfound confidence and healthier relationship with my body impacted how I felt with a camera in my hand as I walked around the ship dining room and politely asked passengers to allow themselves to be photographed, "That's right, lean in a bit, lovely and thank you." The new strength in my legs affected my walks around Napoli and Reykjavik and Corsica and Zakynthos. My growing sense of optimism and relief at having been able to accomplish minor fitness goals allowed me to see Venice and Casablanca and St. Petersburg with more clarity, helped me to sit down in the crew mess and explore new foods that I trusted myself to keep down, liquids at first because something about solid food sitting in my stomach was still too disturbing. I sipped on soups, and ate yogurts, and little by little began to introduce other rapidly dissolving foods like tiny pieces of toast or crackers, my daily runs bringing to me a sense of peace that with each day pulled me further and further away from the crew bar and closer to *la solución*.

Running kept me calm when I started to worry about life after cruise ships, for as much as I loved the experience of getting paid to see the world, I knew my tiny cabin with no porthole was not a final destination. Running provided me with structure when I got off the MV *Oriana* and stayed for a few months with my boyfriend's family in Tamworth, England; running helped me relax when I returned home to Miami, my suitcase packed with souvenirs but still no life plan, anxiety rearing its ugly head whenever someone asked, "What are you going to do now?"

Running helped to silence my racing thoughts when again I found myself pouring drinks behind a busy bar, this time at the newly opened Hard Rock Café in downtown Miami, my college degree sitting on a metaphorical shelf in my brain as I went for long runs down Old Cutler Road, a beautiful tree-lined avenue on which majestic, straight out of a *telenovela* homes sat on each side. These rain or shine runs would often end at Matheson Hammock Park on the bay, a slice of heaven in which I would indulge whenever anxiety and fear and worry threatened to consume me. *What are you doing with your life? What are you doing with your life? What are you doing with your life? What now? What now? What now?*

Mami and Papi were happy to have me home again, and although I was grateful for the comfort of my own bed and space, too soon I found myself struggling with the monster that was Mami's obsession with the impending tragedies that would befall me the minute I walked out the door. With my mind trying to keep a grip on hope and optimism for the future, I would walk out the door, Mami reminding me to be careful because I could get shot while sitting in traffic, kidnapped while running, assaulted at the *gasolinera*, pummeled with a machete at the nail salon, her words coming from a good place but inevitably chipping away at the positive mindset that I wanted badly to be a permanent thing.

I had always perceived my parents as people who had taken great risks and made many sacrifices to give us a better life, envisioned them as *superhumans* because without courage, Papi wouldn't have sailed away from Cuba on a stolen boat in the middle of the night, and Mami wouldn't have crossed the border into a country in which success was not guaranteed for an uneducated immigrant with no grasp of English. That they were constantly afraid of what might happen to me was at odds with their own actions and with my beliefs about them as people, annoying me in the worst of ways.

Their well-intentioned advice landed on me with a heavy thud, their suggestions heavily influenced by bits and pieces of information they'd heard from someone who knew someone else who read it in some obscure newspaper, their words grinding on my nerves like nails on a chalkboard.

"Running too much is bad for you."

"You shouldn't drink so much tea."

"I heard on the news that you shouldn't wash your hair every day."

"I read in the paper that you shouldn't drink too much water."

"My friend at the barber shop told me you shouldn't go to that park."

"There was a story in the news about a woman who lost her uterus because she was exercising too much."

Whereas Mami reminded me of all the ways in which I might die, Papi's suggestions leaned more toward career choices. He kept to his promise and never told me how to live my life, choosing instead to drop hints here and there. "I heard US immigration is hiring and government jobs have great benefits . . ." hints rooted in the hopes that I would achieve the things for which they'd worked so hard: *security, stability, and safety*. His words fell on deaf ears because I wanted him to encourage me to take risks and continue exploring, to find a vocation that would fill my heart rather than my savings account. The idea that I should get a job for the sake of a steady income and good benefits frustrated me, their inability to understand what I wanted saddened me, for my dream was not so much to find safety but instead to honor their sacrifices by taking advantage of the opportunities they'd laid at my feet the moment I'd burst into the world, to explore my freedom, take greater risks, dream bigger dreams, and go farther and accomplish so much more than a steady paycheck and a retirement plan.

Yet no matter how much I disagreed with Papi, I needed his approval of me. Guilt weighed on me for not having found a forever career; prioritizing fulfillment and happiness over stability and safety kept me up at night. Making over three hundred dollars a night at the Hard Rock Café and being able to save money made me feel worse, not better, the idea that I was wasting my college degree, and wasting my time, and wasting my life adding to the gigantic chip on my shoulder that I'd been carrying since I'd walked across the stage and collected my college diploma.

My future seemed less certain each time Mami or Papi handed me a piece of mail and asked me to read it. "We don't understand what it says." Their reliance on me as the person who could fix anything became heavier with each day as I called the cable company to change their channel lineup, called the phone company to question their bill, called the airline to check on flights to Mexico. Their sudden dependency confused me because I wondered how on Earth they'd managed to get things done when I was a child. Never in a million years could I say no to my parents when they asked me for help, and I did get a sense of satisfaction each time I was able to *resolver* a problem, but all the same it stressed me to no end and made me worry that I would wind up living with them for the rest of my life, forced to watch *Caso Cerrado* and The Discovery Channel for all eternity.

This period of my life found me developing new ways to handle stress and anxiety, my unhealthy choices rationalized by running, the great equalizer that justified the nine beers on a Wednesday night at Tobacco Road and the intermittent episodes of bingeing and purging. Buckets of foul-smelling sweat poured out of me as I ran to alleviate guilt and tame the awful pressure to figure things out, my feet striking the pavement in a steady rhythm as I longed to connect with the other version of me that I'd discovered on that first treadmill, the determined, strong, and resilient version of me I'd found somewhere between three minutes and five miles. For as empowered as I'd felt coming off the MV *Oriana*, something about moving back in with my parents and going back to bartending had crushed my spirit and made me doubt myself, made me wonder if perhaps I was stupid for wanting to

accomplish more, silly for trying to find purpose and passion instead of safety and security. *Why can't you be happy?
What's wrong with you? What's wrong with you?* . . . the
endless runs down Old Cutler Road simply not enough
to stop me from bingeing and purging altogether, not
enough to quell the fear that I would never find out what
life wanted from me.

IMPOSTER SYNDROME

"DOES IT LOOK RIGHT?" I ASKED. "SHOULD I MOVE IT over a little bit? What about this one? Should we move it over to the other side?"

"Grab that big one and move it a little bit to the right . . . a little bit more . . . okay, right there. *Perfect.*"

As kids, Raz and I would constantly shift the Christmas presents under the tree, inch them this way and that, my obsession with perfection not an isolated phenomenon. Like me, Raz was dedicated to the notion that our Christmas tree had to look movie/postcard/jigsaw puzzle/ Norman Rockwell painting kind of perfect, both of us having watched *Happy Days* and *The Brady Bunch* religiously and having concluded that Christmas wouldn't feel right unless our tree looked like the ones in American homes. With determination and focus, we arranged and rearranged the gifts under the tree on a weekly and sometimes daily basis to make sure that each present, ornament, lightbulb, and piece of tinsel was in the right place so that we could feel like real *Americanos.*

But the presence of a Christmas tree in our living room was really the only thing American about our traditions, our culture having established long before we were born that the birth of Jesus was to be celebrated on Christmas Eve, aka *Noche Buena,* an occasion during which we were often dragged to adult gatherings, every child thrown into a bedroom with toys and board games, Raz and I inevitably falling asleep on a couch or chair or dog bed. Mami would gently shake us awake to take us home, "Wake up, *ya nos vamos.*" Our parents slightly inebriated, they would let us open all of our gifts at one in the morning because we couldn't restrain ourselves, American traditions be damned.

Still, I never stopped hoping that someday we'd open presents on Christmas morning, that we'd eat French toast instead of day-old toasted Cuban bread smothered in butter and sugar. I longed to wear a sweater, drink hot chocolate, and play in the snow rather than hang out in shorts and a T-shirt, sweat drops forming along my upper lip as I sipped on *café con leche*, any hopes of sitting down for a proper Christmas dinner dashed as we'd pile into our 1974 Caprice Classic and drive all over Miami to visit with relatives and *amistades* who made sure we had enough Maja Soap, Cella's Chocolate Covered Cherries, and Holiday Life Saver Storybooks to last us into old age.

One *Noche Buena* not long after we moved to Miami, I woke up earlier than Raz and ran into the dining room hoping to take ownership of the television and watch *A Charlie Brown Christmas*, my chubby legs screeching to a halt as I came face to face with a gigantic dead pig lying face up on the dining room table, its body split open and spread wide on a wooden plank and seasoned top to bottom, the smell of bitter orange, lemon, garlic, and salt so overpowering that I temporarily stopped breathing and screamed, "Maaaaaaaaaaaaamiiiiiiiiiiiiiiiiiii!"

It was nothing at all to be worried about, apparently, just a Cuban tradition to which we'd never been exposed in California, a super normal, very regular, and absolutely essential part of the *Noche Buena* tradition, a lump in my throat forming as Papi slowly explained to me the entire process. "*Mija, tranquila,* we shot it at the farm, and it's been dead for a long time." The visual of my father shooting a pig and driving it back to the house in the back of a pick-up truck made it all worse. Nausea overwhelmed me as I watched Papi and some random Cuban dude carry the pig outside and place it inside a *caja china*, a wooden death box in which the pig would roast for no less than twelve hours, after which the guests would stab the dead creature with a fork and argue over who would get the snout or the tongue or the tail. My complete refusal to eat *lechón* with rice and black beans was at first met with disapproval and confusion. "But it's so delicious, *mija*, just try *un poquito*." My vision for an American Christmas was momentarily forgotten when someone handed me a chunk of crispy pork skin, a delicacy that smelled entirely too good to pass up. "Oh my God, that is soooo yummy." Papi and his shotgun approach to securing our *Noche Buena* dinner was completely forgiven as I licked my fingers and walked outside to get another piece of crispy pork skin.

Thanksgiving was no different. Our desire for turkey was not strong enough to convince Mami and Papi to forgo their dedication to *lechón* until the year we actually convinced Mami to try her hand at a turkey, a project she undertook with love just to pacify us, our sights set on a normal Thanksgiving until we realized that Mami had soaked the turkey overnight in Mojo sauce and had stuffed it with *arroz congrí* instead of Stove Top stuffing, the mashed potatoes and green bean casserole replaced by fried sweet plantains and boiled cassava as though we didn't eat these foods the other three-hundred sixty-four days of the year, our almost-American Thanksgiving made complete by the two flans we shared for dessert because Papi had taken advantage of a buy-one-get-one-free deal at Sedanos Supermarket. My childhood dreams of fully experiencing an American life may have been one reason I eventually moved to Orlando, a smaller city not far from Miami in geographical terms but worlds apart in a hundred million ways.

I'd been living at home with Mami and Papi for over a year, the ongoing *críticas* and manic attention to *Al Rojo Vivo* and *Noticias Telemundo* having made a serious dent in my ability to remain calm, my temper short and irritability through the roof. I'd remained close with Lisa, my friend from TGI Fridays, but complaining to her about my unhappiness was not an option, not when I'd just spent the last few years onboard a cruise ship and traveling to places most people never got to see in their lifetime. I'd written only a few letters to Father Gabriel, and even though I knew God was all merciful and Jesus still loved me, I was too ashamed to look Father Gabriel in the eye, too afraid he would notice that my quads and calf muscles were the only parts of me that had grown in any way.

I found some level of comfort in Papi, the person who always made me feel better whenever I had a problem, the one who encouraged me to believe that nothing was impossible, *todo tiene solución*, for he believed that to every problem there was a solution be it a flat tire, a lost wallet, a stolen car, a missing purse, a toothache, menstrual cramps, or the flu.

But Papi still knew nothing about my racing thoughts, *I can't stop thinking*. The tightness in my chest, *I can't breathe*. The irritability that made me bitchy, *I hate everything*. My daily runs were simply not enough to chill me out; anger and fear and frustration brewed inside of me until it reached a boiling point and I snapped. Mami's jaw hit the kitchen floor as I yelled at the top of my lungs, all of my frustration spilling out of me. "*Coño*, why can't you just say something positive? I'm so tired of always feeling like this! It's so dark in here and depressing and negative, and you're always watching the news, and can we please just leave the blinds open for once!"

Papi had just gotten home from work, his body dripping in sweat and eyes widening to hear me disrespecting Mami, his initial anger and shock then diffused by the look on my face, by the realization that I was clearly unhinged and *nerviosa*, that I was trying to breathe but failing, my hands trembling and tears running down my face. "I think I need help. I think I need medication. I'm not feeling good. Something is wrong with me. I'm not okay. I'm not okay. I'm not okay." Papi's concern then turned into consternation as he shook his head slowly, "No no no, you don't need *ningún medicamento*, you just need rest."

Assuming something concrete must have happened to me, they asked me questions for which I had no answers. "*¿Qué pasó?* Did someone hurt you? Is it work?"

"Nothing happened," I said, crying hard but not able to say, "I'm scared and worried and angry and frustrated and I feel like a failure because I don't know what I'm doing with my life." Their concerns were alleviated only after I reassured them that I wasn't on drugs and hadn't been raped or kidnapped or assaulted. Silence filled the little kitchen, pierced only by the sound of my hiccups as I tried to get it together, my parents logically worried about me but not enough to suggest therapy or medication.

Wiping my face with the sleeve of my T-shirt, I went to my room to *descansar* and hopefully stop feeling shaky and unstable, a few hours of rest that served me because the silence gave birth to an idea that brought me some relief. *I need to move,* I thought. *Miami traffic sucks, and people are so rude, and it's noisy and loud and frustrating, and I'm still living at home, and I'm not going anywhere, and I just want to live someplace different.* The city of Miami took the blame for my unhappiness because I hadn't known to connect it to the brokenness inside of me, the idea of moving away creating an illusion of happiness because I believed spreading my wings again would help me find *la solución.*

The idea that I could live in my own space and keep the blinds open and watch anything other than the news started to take shape. A few days was all it took for me to make a decision to move to Orlando, a city where I knew a handful of people and to where I could transfer my job at the Hard Rock Café, a place far enough away to achieve independence, but not so far that I couldn't drive home.

I'd visited Orlando a handful of times for the pleasure of going to Disney World and Epcot, experiences that had been brief but long enough to convince me that Orlando was super different, Miami having become a gigantic concrete jungle of endless strip malls with small businesses that thought nothing of advertising in Spanish, *Envíos a Cuba, Angelito Farmacia, Barbería Pepe,* the green grass and shrubs in front of many homes ripped out and replaced with cement driveways unless you lived in super-uppity Coral Gables, where a permit was needed to whisper let alone change the front lawn to concrete. What little I'd seen of Orlando was so starkly different from Miami that I believed it would be an *America, Here I Come* experience.

Papi had been happy for my opportunity to see some of the world on cruise ships, but my decision to move out and pay rent confused him. "*Pero aquí tienes tu casa*." The advice he'd given me to be independent was overshadowed by his broken heart, his words coming back to haunt him as Mami helped me pack my belongings into my car along with four rolls of toilet paper, a container of *arroz con pollo*, two avocados and three mangos, her expression worried and sad as she slipped a twenty-dollar bill into my hand, *por si las moscas*. For a brief moment, I felt horribly conflicted, some part of me recognizing that my unhappiness was nobody's fault, least of all hers, the realization that I'd been mean to her and unfair nearly causing a breakdown. "I love you, Mami." I gave her tiny frame a quick hug lest I lose my resolve and change my mind.

I pushed all thoughts of Mami and Papi out of my mind and fantasized about my new life, adrenaline coursing through me as I headed north on the Florida Turnpike, fully convinced that living alone, making new friends, and working a new job would finally make me happy.

Maybe I'll find my dream job, I thought. I hoped something meaningful and impactful would land on my lap, and this recurrent desire to be part of something bigger than me was the reason I took a job as a permanent substitute teacher at Ocoee Middle School, where an assistant principal took notice of me and planted an idea in my brain: "You're good with kids. You can be a full-time teacher with your college degree"—an idea that struck a chord because I was done with cleaning ashtrays and working nights and restocking beer, tired of feeling like I wasn't living up to my potential, the three-hundred-plus miles I'd driven north having added more weight and size to the already huge chip on my shoulder.

I interviewed with the principal of Howard Middle

School, a kind African American man who believed I'd be a good fit for the students in the At-Risk program. His assumption of my success was based not on my college education but on my ethnicity and culture. "I think they'll appreciate that you're Latino." The realities of the job and the challenges I would face were completely lost on me because in truth I was more excited about having a "real" job than about effecting change; this new job with a steady paycheck and benefits temporarily quashed my internal angst, it being a career that would make my parents proud and justify my decision to move away.

I'm finally an adult, I thought, and I proceeded to do everything considered "normal" by the standards of my social environment and by what I'd read in books and seen in movies. Working at the Hard Rock Café had exposed me to peers with whom I'd established pseudo-friendships based on mutual interests like running and bike rides. Opportunities to socialize were common, helping to connect me to more people, to young professionals my age making twice my salary as a teacher, groups of white people who looked much like the cast of *Friends*, their mannerisms and clothing and backgrounds a glimpse into another world in which I'd never set foot and was excited to explore. I'd traveled to many different countries and had been exposed to numerous cultures and ethnicities, but never had I lived in a city in which there were more white people than Latinos, my ethnicity thus becoming a topic of conversation that usually went something like this:

"You're half Mexican? You don't *look* Mexican."

"What does that mean?" I'd want to say.

"You're half Cuban? You don't *look* Cuban."

"What does that mean?" I'd want to say.

"You were born in the United States? It's amazing that you speak English without an accent."

"What?"

"You went to college? Wow, good for you."

"Seriously?"

These comments bothered me, but such was my desire to feel accepted and validated by my white counterparts that I never advocated for myself, never questioned these ridiculous comments that spoke to their level of ignorance and lack of education, this pressure to be more like them leading me to shrug off their comments and make irrational decisions that made it harder for me to develop my own identity. My very long, curly hair was chopped off, my new haircut based solely on the recommendation of the wildly flamboyant and lovable gay man who took one look at me and said, "That hair is sooo ten years ago. Let's do something about that, shall we?" I bought an expensive car, rented a nicer apartment in a brand-new complex in Metro-West, and spent money on furnishings to make it look picture perfect on the inside. Having been limited to uniform pants and shirts for years, I bought clothes that seemed appropriate for the world in which I lived, my credit card filling up with charges from The Limited and Banana Republic, my new wardrobe and hair aimed at making me pass for a successful young woman who was going places. And to places I certainly went: book signings, art exhibitions, and outdoor concerts, my outward appearance always fitting the occasion because if I looked the part, then clearly the happiness would follow.

Only it never really did, no amount of perfection in any area of my life able to quash the awful feeling that I was lying all the time, that I was pretending my way through life, trying to convince myself that I was complete, that I had arrived, that I was finally *there*. Not only was I *not there*, I was consequently drowning in debt given the tragedy that was my teacher's salary and my irrational spending on things I couldn't afford. "Don't worry, I'll pay the tab."

Each time I went home for a weekend, I painted the picture I thought Mami and Papi wanted to see. Their eyes lit up to hear that I'd secured a job as a schoolteacher. Their smiles then faded when they learned that I'd quit the teaching job and had found a new job at a bank in which I was making more money. Papi took a long drag on a cigarette when I told him I'd quit my job at the bank, his gaze skeptical as I told him about the nice man I'd helped at the bank who'd invited me to interview for his company, Bristol Hotels. And although the new job was even more *dinero* and good benefits, after three job changes, Papi couldn't help but be worried. "It's not good to keep switching jobs, *mija,* you need to settle down." But I couldn't settle down, couldn't fall in love with any one job because none of them felt like the right fit, the perfect shoe, the mother of all of dream jobs.

Pressure and fear weighed on me as I drank my way around the city of Orlando, laughing and pretending to be in love with my life as I downed pints of beer at Scruffy Murphy's and Katie O'Brien's, my feet striking the hot asphalt as I ran every day under the hot sun, hoping to turn a corner and find happiness waiting for me because living over three hundred miles away from home had not brought me any closer to *la solución*, only further. Whereas I'd wanted to find my dream job and to feel a sense of purpose, I'd traded that in for the sake of more money and better benefits.

For safety and security.

Far be it for me to tell Mami and Papi how truly lost and alone I felt; the last thing I wanted was for them to worry about me from so far away. Mami would agonize from sunup to sunset, and Papi would lose sleep if he knew that I was paying for groceries with my credit card. I'd done a great job of pretending to have my shit together, and I couldn't imagine ruining their perception of me.

Instead of telling them the truth, I went home to visit as much as I could, at first tentative to believe that I was homesick and eventually realizing that for as much as I'd wanted a different life, I missed desperately all the things I'd once blamed for my unhappiness: the endless strip malls, the chaos that is the Palmetto Expressway and the drivers who don't know how to use a turn signal, "*Coño, acere,* learn to drive, bro!" I longed to drive down the tree-lined avenues in Coral Gables and run over the Rickenbacker Causeway Bridge against the backdrop of a beautiful sunset; I missed the tiny cafeterias bustling with energy and noise along *Calle Ocho* and how, no matter the time of day, I could get a *medianoche* sandwich or a *café con leche;* I missed the way the entire city smells of *lechón* on Christmas Eve and how Spanish is the language of choice; I missed the music, whatever hate I'd had for salsa and merengue as a teenager long forgotten. Many times, as I headed home after a weekend with my parents, I would tune in to a Spanish radio station, the music of Oscar D'León or Joe Arroyo or Marc Anthony serving as a buffer for the loneliness I would feel once I returned to my small one-bedroom apartment in Orlando.

Yet more than the music and the food and the traffic,

I missed the spirit of *mi gente*, the deep soul of Miami, a vibe that could only be generated by the many incredible people who'd emigrated from the Caribbean, Central and South America, each one having brought with them a desire for a better life, a chance to *avanzar*, an opportunity to provide for their children a life so much better than their own, all of their sweat and tears and strength combined generating the warmth and zest for life that I felt each time my car slipped out of Broward County and straight into the 3-0-5, Miami-Dade County. *Home.*

I missed my parents and most of all, my Cuban family, having recognized that for all their *críticas* and brutal honesty, they loved me all the same and I them. My anger and resentment and frustration as a teenager was valid and real, but it would never be strong enough to change the fact that blood is thicker than water and love always wins.

Yet no matter how much I ached for home, I could not share with my family to what degree I felt alone, sad, and in despair, could not expose them to the truth, could not tell them that perhaps the source of my unhappiness lay not within the city of Miami, but within me.

No matter where you go, there you are.

Being an imposter took a toll. I started to run less often, the resulting weight gain leading me right back to regular bingeing and purging. My social engagements came to a halt as I withdrew into myself little by little, my inability to sleep through the night prompting me to start taking Advil PM, the medication having more effect when swallowed with a glass or two of red wine, the perpetual fog in my brain getting in the way of clarity, a tornado of dark thoughts swirling in my head one night as I opened a new bottle of pills. *I'm broke. I'm afraid. I'm in debt. I'm a loser. I'm a sell-out*—all of it consuming me as I considered swallowing all of the pills. *Fuck it.* A vision of Mami and Papi brought tears to my eyes because I was failing to honor their many *sacrificios*, disrespecting Papi's calloused hands and the years of poverty and hunger that Mami had suffered as a child, failing to be the daughter they'd hoped for. *Maybe I should have stuck with piano.* That I would consider taking my own life scared me, the idea that I would be better off dead a good indicator that I needed to pick up the phone and let someone know that I was *really not okay.*

Raz answered the phone on the first ring, my sobbing enough for him to realize that indeed, I was really not okay. "I can't . . . I'm just . . . sad . . . I'm so . . . sad . . . I need help . . ." the genuine concern I heard on the other end of the phone exactly what I needed to calm down and formulate a rational thought based on nothing but the truth.

"I think I need to go home," I said, a decision that triggered the same relief I'd felt three years prior when I'd moved to Orlando, the pressure and stress of living a complete lie not worth my life. All of my belongings were packed up and loaded into the U-Haul that Mami and Papi would drive home. My way-too-expensive car headed south on the Florida Turnpike, my eyes on a beautiful sunset as I wondered if I'd ever *resolver* the shit storm within me.

SINGLE AND BADASS

MY DETERMINATION TO BE SUPER INDEPENDENT HAD propelled me to move to Orlando in the first place, and it had kept me aloof and indifferent to serious relationships for most of my young adult life, that is until I moved back to Miami in the throes of depression. No sooner had we parked the U-Haul in front of my parents' home did I get bombarded with comments from family and nosy neighbors, endless *críticas* that rattled my *nervios* and shook the already unstable foundation on which I was standing.

"Yvonne! You're looking healthy (kiss). *¿Tienes novio?*"

"*Hola, mi amor* (kiss) *¿Y no te has casado?* What about a boyfriend?"

"*Yvonnecita,* (kiss), *que bueno* that you moved back home, and the extra weight looks good on you. *Oye,* when are you getting married?"

I'd always thought being single was cool, but at twenty-seven years old and once again living with my parents, I began to doubt my belief, question my stubborn refusal to settle down. I was back in Miami and surrounded by young Latinas who squealed whenever someone got engaged—"Let me see the ring!", a recurrent phenomenon that made me uneasy on many levels, this discomfort made worse by the unsolicited advice from women who took it upon themselves to question my indifference to weddings, my decision to remain single and childless interpreted as an insult to the entire Cuban population. "*Óyeme,* if you wait too long, all the good ones will be taken. Find a good guy and marry him, *porque si no,* you'll end up alone." The ongoing discourse was inescapable, a phenomenon that I witnessed at work, in my spin class, at the grocery store, in bars, at networking events. "*Pero* like did you see Maria's ring? It's, like, super beautiful and, like, she told me *que* they're having the reception at the Biltmore Hotel and going to Bora Bora or *algo así,* I don't know. I'm telling you, Carlos better get his act together, *porque* like I'm not going to have kids when I'm forty and like, for sure for sure I wanna get married at Church of the Little Flower in Coral Gables *porque* it's so beautiful . . ."

Ever since my disastrous relationship with The One, I'd been fiercely opposed to marriage and children, but that didn't stop me from dating and playing the field. I had a few casual boyfriends over the years, and Mami got her hopes up each time I'd brought home a new boyfriend: "He looks like a nice guy, *mija*." But whatever hopes she had for a wedding and grandchildren slowly faded as one by one I tore through the hearts of guys who made the sad mistake of falling in love with me, such as the guy from upstate New York I'd met while working at Fridays, an angel of a friend who would've moved mountains for me and had often tried: "I'm sorry but I don't want to ruin our friendship."

The English guy from cruise ships: "I'm sorry but this will never work."

The firefighter from Connecticut: "I can't do long distance."

The wealthy Cuban guy in his BMW and expensive clothes that I did an excellent job of scaring away: "You don't want to be with someone like me."

The guys in Orlando with whom I shared my physical body but never the inner workings of my heart: "I'm not looking for love."

The young man from Argentina who made me laugh constantly but with whom I didn't see a future: "I can't do this."

They were all super nice guys who'd believed me to be confident and fierce and grounded because that's the picture I'd painted for them, but it had always come to, "No thanks, I don't need anyone." Mami eventually stopped making comments about my love life, having grown accustomed to hearing me say, "Forget about it. I am never getting married. I am never having children."

Never say never.

I'd proudly worn my Single and Badass badge, and held on to my *warrior* persona for years, even though she had clearly fallen apart and sunk into a severe depression all by her badass self. But the badge no longer seemed as cool, because something about living at home only a few months shy of my twenty-eighth birthday made me question and doubt everything. *Is it wrong that I want to be alone? What if I don't get married, and then I wake up one day regretting it? What if all the good guys are taken by the time I decide to get married? What if I get too old to have kids? Do I want kids? What if I marry someone who doesn't like to travel? What if he tries to control me?* The doubts swirling in my brain made it hard to concentrate, and rather than explore them and find the truth, I found myself referring back to the narrative that had always brought me a sense of safety and order. *I don't need anyone. I am strong. I am independent. I am my own person*—thoughts that tricked me into thinking I should move out of my parents' house once again, less than one year after I'd moved back home, the only improvement in my life the considerable dent

I'd made in my mountain of debt because seeing a therapist or taking medication had not been an option. The tiny apartment I found on South Beach was a short-lived safe harbor for the shipwreck that was my mental health, because even though I had no business venturing into a serious relationship, I made space for a new boyfriend one month after I moved into my tiny apartment a few blocks from the beach: a lovely Englishman with blue eyes who'd agreed with the plan to move in together even though we hadn't known each other for very long.

He was a free-spirited artist and photographer whom I met at my corporate job, our mutual distaste of the corporate world helping to cement our bond, the novelty of a super grown-up relationship sweeping me away. In the beginning, we talked about our dreams of traveling and being free from quotas, emails, and meetings—mutual visions that we discussed at length over endless bottles of red wine and cigarettes. I felt relief at having found a kindred spirit, which made it easy to ignore the calories in the Manchego cheese and imported salami we shared most nights as we planned our lives together, the extra weight on my stomach, hips, and thighs escaping my attention, my ability to shrug off the fact that my pants were getting tighter a message that perhaps I really was in love. Perhaps.

I brought him home to meet my family. Charmed by his lovely accent and the respect with which he treated everyone, Mami whispered into my ear, "I like him very much, *mija*. I have a feeling about him." Her comment made me smile, because I wanted nothing more than to make my parents proud, to prove to them that their daughter wasn't a complete disaster, that I would never again need rescuing.

The *guerrera* inside of me tried desperately to remain afloat, but I ignored her. Family members asked me constantly if we were going to get married, and although the prospect made my stomach cramp, I calmed down by reminding myself that perhaps it was time to bury the free-spirited warrior, to settle down and look to having a family, to stop obsessing over finding my dream job.

My blunt refusal to consider the truth blinded me to all the warning signs. I didn't stop to consider that everything was moving entirely too fast, didn't worry that I'd never fully explored the reasons why I'd fallen into a severe depression, didn't care that I was drinking and smoking every single night and sneaking away to the bathroom whenever I'd felt like I'd eaten a little too much, didn't wonder why I sometimes had to take deep breaths for absolutely no reason or why achieving any kind of happiness wasn't possible unless I was slightly inebriated or running five miles.

And because I didn't see all the reasons why I should pause and reflect and question and explore, I found myself standing before my lovely Englishman less than a year later, my heart beating wildly and palms sweating as I said the words, "I do."

JUMPING OFF THE TRAIN

"MIJA, HOW IS EVERYTHING WITH YOUR MARIDO? ARE you happy that you're married?"

Mami and I were sitting in a booth at Pizza Hut, one of her favorite places to eat. I was flirting with my slice of pizza, hoping Mami wouldn't notice that I was still not comfortable eating certain foods.

"Yes, Mami, I'm happy," I lied.

"*Ah, que bueno*," she said, taking a huge bite of pizza with her tiny mouth. "See? I was right when I told you I had a feeling about him."

Mami had not been alone in her "feeling" as I, too, had felt something when we'd applied for a marriage license at Miami Beach City Hall, my feeling more like a pit in my stomach, a horrible premonition that things would not work out, but like a *pendeja*, I'd done it anyway, too afraid to back out because Mami and Papi had been so happy, my entire family rejoicing that I was not a lesbian, as though loving another woman was a horrible affliction, "*Coño*, we all thought you were gay!"

With such an amazing send-off and so many people convinced we'd found true love, I wanted to believe my "feeling" had been cold feet, a normal occurrence for any bride or groom, and I told myself I knew what I was doing.

Only at twenty-nine years old, I didn't know shit.

Sitting across from Mami at Pizza Hut, the only thing I knew for certain was that something was terribly wrong, and that I had no idea how to find *la solución*. Telling them I wasn't sure I liked being married would've been an insult to them, and I worried they would think they'd failed to provide me with a good foundation. Plus, I worried the "scandal" would crush Mami. Raz had gotten married years before I did, and when he'd chosen to get a divorce, Mami had been mortified.

"*Ay Dios mio*," she'd said. "Please don't tell anyone your brother got a divorce. It's better if nobody knows."

Divorce was a dirty word that my parents never uttered to each other nor to anyone else, their commitment to marriage making me feel guilty and shameful for not being happy with the young man whose gentle demeanor and cool accent had all the promise of a *Notting Hill*-type of romance.

Mami looked at me as though reading my thoughts and sensing the doubts circulating within me. I looked away and made like I was looking for the waitress. "*Mija*," she said, the concern in her voice impossible to ignore, "do you love him? Tell me the truth, *¿estás enamorada de verdad?*"

It's very possible that I was in love with him, but whatever I felt was being buried under intense fear because love had once proved dangerous and scary, had resulted in heartbreak and sadness. Love meant that I would have to be just like Mami, that I would have to set aside my own needs for the sake of others and be fine with second place. For all I knew he was The One, version two-point-zero, but I still wasn't one-hundred percent sure. He had many great qualities, but the butterflies in my stomach and that magical spell from long ago had never returned, and doubting everything made me feel guilty and flawed.

What's wrong with you, Yvonne? I would think. *Why can't you be happy?*

Happiness would never be possible, because clearly I'd buckled under the pressure to keep up with my counterparts, to be the daughter I thought my parents wanted, to do at least one thing right with my life given I'd failed at finding a forever job, my determination to find the unicorn of all careers having led to abrupt resignations from well-paying jobs for the sake of finding my purpose. I'd been a bartender, a cruise ship purser and photographer, a teacher, a financial analyst, a hotel salesperson, and an operations manager, jobs that had offered me security and safety but never the golden ticket: fulfillment.

Someday you will know what this life wants from you.

Given Mami and Papi's examples, I believed that being married meant I had to give up my dream of finding purpose, and instead focus on having children. Hearing the concern in Mami's voice, I wondered if she'd be able to set aside her devotion for my Englishman and hear me out. She grabbed the remaining slices of pizza, wrapped them in a paper napkin and put them in her purse.

"Mami, they have boxes for the pizza. You don't have to do that."

"No, *mija*, it's okay," perhaps afraid she'd never again see the pizza once it left the table. "*Entonces*, do you love him?"

Her face held all the reasons why I couldn't tell her the truth; I saw the fear in her eyes, the sadness in her slight frown, the way her tiny upper body seemed to cave in on itself as though to prepare for bad news.

I gave her the biggest smile I could muster. "*Of course*, Mami," I lied, "he's my husband, how could I not be in love with him? He's such a good guy."

She sat up instantly and smiled, obviously relieved.

"That makes me very happy. He's such a nice *muchacho, mija*. I like him very much, and so does your Papi."

"Uh-huh," I said, my hopes for a woman-to-woman conversation crushed.

"Don't forget, *mija*," she said as she leaned forward, "your duty is to your husband. Make sure you cook for him, keep everything clean, and iron his *camisetas*."

I wanted to do no such thing, but my strong Latino upbringing and the expectations attached were not to be ignored, the pressure to be a good wife the reason I let Mami teach me how to cook *arroz con pollo* and *picadillo*. I wanted badly to find my own way of expressing love, but Mami's words haunted me: "*Tu deber es a tu marido*," your duty is to your husband. Guilt and anxiety plagued me whenever I did anything for myself; I felt bad whenever I went for a run or spent hours at the gym, my battles with food and my body having returned in full force after I'd seen cellulite on my legs and sagging skin on my arms, whatever balance I'd achieved thrown out the window.

Guilt was not enough to stop me from letting obsessive exercise become my new addiction, the three hours I spent in the gym plus the two hours at the Shotokan Karate school I'd joined the only things that made me feel strong and fierce, emotions I clung to because although our life seemed picture perfect, the awful premonition became a loud voice that gave me little peace. *This is all wrong.* Our brief marriage would eventually crash and burn because I'd clipped the wings shortly after we'd taken off, and my own life would continue on a collision course as I single-handedly destroyed my next two relationships.

As always, the *guerrera* encouraged me to *Be strong. Don't cry*—to ignore whatever I was feeling and push forward, my determination to find fulfillment the reason I gave up another great job as a linguist for the Department of Justice and decided to become a certified personal trainer, a decision that logically confused my parents but made perfect sense to me even though I was near bankrupt and nowhere near emotionally stable. Within months I was one of the busiest trainers at a luxury health club in Miami Beach, my troubles with money at last coming to an end as I worked my way into a Personal Training Manager position and moved into a new apartment.

Sad, tired, drained, nervous, anxious, scared, worried—none of these emotions stopped me from thinking that still I had a purpose for my life, but the irony of this career choice was not lost on me. No number of squats or lunges or push-ups could stop me from recognizing the hypocrisy of my double life: *You're a fraud. You're an imposter. You're a liar!* It mattered little how much I loved my new job; I couldn't shake the awful feeling that I was not okay.

Still, that I had found a profession that brought me joy and fulfillment provided me with the space I needed to breathe, gave me the courage to get off the metaphorical train on which I'd jumped and to recognize that perhaps I'd been the driver all along. Tentatively, I explored this new space in the privacy of my apartment, the sound of my breath piercing the silence, no wine or cigarettes to help me because I had decided to give myself a fair shot, had realized that rather than *cope* with my life, I wanted to *live* it, and perhaps find what life really wanted from me.

One day, I sat on my couch and thought of Father Gabriel, the young priest who'd shown me kindness, compassion, and understanding, the memory of that day surfacing in my mind as I closed my eyes. *Please, God. Please, God. Please, God.* Only I didn't pray for a *solución*, but rather for the courage to be honest, for as much time as I'd spent inside my head, I'd never moved past my thoughts and into my emotions; I'd tried to out-drink, out-run, and out-exercise every ounce of sadness, anxiety, anger, fear, and frustration, this awful pattern coming to an end as I heard the voice of a girl who'd stuck two fingers down her throat and flushed her self-esteem and confidence down the toilet.

What is the truth, Yvonne?

LA SOLUCIÓN

"Is it ready, mami? I'm so hungry." I was hunched over, my little face peering into the oven to check on my Chicken Pot Pie, my favorite after school snack.

"Let me see," Mami said. She opened the oven, poked at the pie with a fork. "Not yet, *mija, le falta*. Maybe ten more minutes."

I stayed in the kitchen with Mami, thinking maybe the time would go quicker if I stalked my treat. The phone rang and Mami picked it up on the second ring. "*¿Aló?*" After a few moments during which I could hear a man's voice on the other end of the line, Mami began to scream and cry, one hand on her heart as she shook her head from side to side. "No no no no no no no no, *ay Dios mío*, no no. *¿Qué me estás diciendo?* What happened to my sister? What happened to Bertha? *No es posible.* Tell me it's not true! No no no no no no no!"

This was the first time in my brief life of ten years that I'd seen Mami come undone. I stood there with my hands on my chubby hips, paralyzed by something—maybe fear, maybe sadness, maybe shock—for Mami had always been a beacon of strength in spite of her *nervios*, a five-foot-tall fireball of a woman who'd once traded harsh words with a nun, a woman who'd never broken down in my presence, not even when I'd knelt down on a nail and screamed and cried in fear, "What if they chop off my leg?" I'd seen Mami anxious, stressed and frustrated, but sad and scared and screaming was a whole new side to her and one that we'd never see again because Mami's emotions were shut down almost instantly, put away for our benefit, hidden and repressed and never again to be expressed because *hay que ser fuerte.*

You have to be strong, so to hell with your grief.

Our neighbor Rosita came over that day and took me and Raz to the flea market, an experience I remember more so because rather than hang out with Rosita, I wanted to be with Mami in her sadness, not away from her. Papi had been adamant that we leave the house, his face a picture of calm as Mami went to the bedroom and spoke to her family in Mexico, the sound of her crying unsettling me long after we got into Rosita's car and drove away. We walked around *el pulguero*, our efforts to cheer Mami up represented in the gift that Rosita bought for her, our understanding of the gesture that it would be something to help Mami get *over* her sadness and grief rather than to process it, because as Mami would be reminded constantly by our family and friends and neighbors, "*Hay que seguir adelante.*"

Life goes on, so to hell with your sadness.

A few years later and for many years after, I would visit with my Abuela Meche and the eight orphaned children my Aunt Bertha left behind when she passed away at thirty-three years old. Although devastated and overcome with grief, my relatives not once cried or expressed sadness or hurt or loneliness or fear in my presence, their emotions repressed for the sake of survival. Instead, those feelings manifested as family conflicts that were beyond my scope of understanding. For all the time I'd spent in Mexico throughout my adolescence and young adulthood, I had never been able to truly comprehend their level of pain and suffering, their subsequent actions and behavior showing me that our family was a tribe of warriors, of *chingonas* with deep wells of inner strength, perseverance, and determination, characteristics and drive that helped them rise out of tremendous poverty and achieve an extraordinary level of financial success, their achievements then chalked up to God's will because "*Solo Dios sabe lo que hace.*"

Still, I would often wonder, *What did they do with their sadness, their grief? Did they forget about it? Did it just go away?*

Not long after my aunt passed away, Papi woke up bright and early one morning and drove to Tamiami Park to pick up my *abuelos* and my uncle, who'd arrived on the Mariel Boat Lift from Cuba. I remember Papi's face that day as he returned with his parents and brother, his joy palpable and no doubt relieved that the risk he'd taken when he sailed away from Cuba had finally paid off: *los abuelos* were safe in America. They lived with us while Papi helped them settle into life in the United States, a life into which my grandfather Erasmo was not able to assimilate, his physical health deteriorating quickly with his diabetes and heart condition and his refusal to stop eating *lechón, arroz blanco,* and *frijoles negros.* He passed away less than two years later, whatever existing relationship between him and my father coming to an abrupt and tragic end, the dreams my father had for a happy reunion *en los Estados Unidos* buried in the grave with his father.

That his father died so soon after arriving was more than enough reason for Papi to break down and cry, to hold up his fist to God in anger and frustration. *¡Coño!* He had every right to express whatever pain he felt as he watched my Abuelo Erasmo being laid to rest in a cemetery only a few miles from our home. But Papi remained to us the same calm, patient man, not once shedding a tear or voicing sadness.

The memory of Mami's loss so fresh on my mind, each day I checked on Papi.

"Papi, are you sad?"

"No, *mija*, I'm okay."

"Papi, do you miss Abuelo?"

"A little bit, *mija*, but it's okay."

Mami told me to stop pestering him, to leave him alone. "He's okay, *mija, no te preocupes,*" her words making no sense on the day that Raz and I ran into the master bedroom and found Mami standing just outside the bathroom, her ear pressed to the door, the look on her face something like fear and worry as she placed a finger to her lips to keep us quiet. My heart shattered to pieces at the sound of Papi's sobs coming from inside the shower, the guttural wails slamming me in the chest and making me cry. Mami turned to see tears running down my face and very quickly ushered me into my bedroom. "No no no no, don't cry, *mija*, don't cry. Your Papi is okay, he's just a little sick today"—words that couldn't erase the visual of Papi crying in the shower, of Papi in tremendous pain and even worse, of Papi all alone with his sadness. Yet when he sat down at the dinner table, he was the man we'd always known, silent and calm as he watched Mami put food on our plates, my concern impossible to hide because he noticed and said, "*¿Y esa cara?* Don't be sad, *mija*. There's no reason to be sad. Let's eat."

I would not consider these experiences and their impact on my ability to fully experience my emotions until I sat alone in my apartment at thirty-five years old, a lifetime of depression, anxiety, bingeing and purging, alcohol abuse, and cigarettes to my name, years of untapped feelings weighing on me as I sat in complete silence, the absence of *something to do* making me uncomfortable, the years of irrational thoughts, unhealthy choices, and poor decisions indicators that I had never known what to do with silence except fill it with self-destructive behaviors.

What is the truth, Yvonne?

The nuns in Catholic school had taught me to tell the truth because lying was a grave sin that hurt Jesus even more than the nails in his hands and feet. That I could hurt Him by telling a lie terrified me as a child and made me worry for me and Mami, because it was from her that I took my cues and developed a perspective of the truth, one that was distorted in such a way that I wondered often if I'd heard wrong when Sister Nancy smacked a little boy in my class on the back of the head and said, "You must never lie."

For example: I was sprawled out on the bedroom floor, playing with my Fisher Price Little People Tree House, at peace with my five-year-old world. Raz was outside setting up a bike ramp that he and his friends had made from scratch, their Huffy and Mongoose bikes laying on the grass underneath the big tree on our front lawn as Mami stood in the kitchen pouring Hawaiian Punch into an ice cube tray.

I was lost in my treehouse adventures when Mami came running into the bedroom, her *nervios* on high alert from head to toe.

"*Mija*, I need you to do me a favor."

I stood up right away. "Okay, Mami."

"When the doorbell rings, open the door and tell Florita that I'm not home."

"But you're home, Mami. I don't understand."

She sighed, exasperated. "I know, but just tell her that I'm not home. That I'll call her later."

Such a simple task, and yet one that caused me great distress, for immediately I started to worry about my promise to Jesus. The doorbell rang, and I bolted for the front door, my little legs running as fast as they could lest I forget the mission.

Florita was standing on the other side of the screen door, smiling down at me as she asked, "*Hola*, Yvonneci-ta, *¿está tu mamá?* Is your mommy home? *Dile que* I came to see her, *ándale*."

I bit my lip, hoping to get it right. "No, she just told me to tell you that she's not home, but she will call you later."

Florita's face clouded over before she turned and walked away, making me wonder if I'd made a mistake. Apparently I had screwed up because Mami came out from where she was hiding and scolded me. "*Ay* Yvonne, why did you tell her that?"

"But I told her what you said, Mami, that you weren't home."

"*Ay Dios mío*," Mami said, "what is she going to think?"

Fast forward a few years, and we find Mami look-ing stressed out and annoyed that a friend of Papi's was coming over for dinner, a Hungarian man that Papi had met on a construction site along with his young wife. "*Ay Dios mío*, give me energy," she'd said as she tried to simul-taneously get the house clean and ready for *una visita*, put together an elaborate dinner, try to put on Lee Press On Nails in between getting dressed and yelling at us to shower and be ready, rivers of sweat pouring down her face and back and soiling her blouse as she checked on the white rice, her frustration and stress boiling over as she noticed that one of her fake nails was missing. "*Ay Dios mío*," she said, "I lost a nail! Yvonne, help me look for it!" We looked all over the kitchen, under the couch, in the bedrooms and the bathrooms, the backyard, inside Spanky's mouth, Mami's *nervios* getting the best of her as the doorbell rang. "*Válgame Dios*," she said, her eyes opening wide to see that two more nails had gotten lost in the shuffle. "And now what do I do? How embarrassing, *qué verguenza.*"

Mami looked disheveled, stressed, and worried as Papi opened the door and welcomed the guests, their bodies rounding the corner and walking into the Florida room just as Mami transformed into another human being altogether: a gracious, polished, calm, beautiful, warm, generous, compassionate, and hilarious hostess who smiled and laughed and told stories and fed them enough food to keep them satiated for a few months, her confidence and self-assuredness not missing a beat even after Papi's friend found one of Mami's nails in his white rice. She laughed and said, "Yvonne was playing with my nails, and she must have dropped one in the pot," her hand finding my leg and pinching me under the table, a reminder to keep the truth to myself.

Again.

Repeatedly, I was reminded to go along with whatever lies were being thrown around:

"Tell them I was sick and couldn't go."

"Tell Georgina to give you a ride home today because my car is in the shop."

"If the phone rings and it's your aunt, tell her I'm not home."

Outright lies that later became more serious:

"Don't tell anyone about your eating disorder."

"Don't tell your cousins you're not a virgin."

"Don't tell anyone you got divorced."

This commitment to perfection and propriety is what Mami had deemed necessary for us to exist in the world and to be accepted, her preoccupation with what other people might think forever guiding her relationship with the truth and instilling in me the belief that it was something to be averted, not welcomed. Judged, not explored.

For many days over the course of one trip around the sun, I would break with tradition and explore the truth as I sat on my couch and prayed, my voice piercing the silence each and every evening, *Please, God. Please, God. Please, God.* The words helped to calm me down when the urges to buy a bottle of wine or binge and purge overwhelmed me. More than the courage to be honest, I prayed for the strength to *be still,* because I'd never done such a thing as lean into my feelings, had never stopped *moving moving moving* and sat alone in a space with nothing to distract me; I deliberately stayed away from TV and music and the internet, *The Holy Bible* and *A New Earth* the only books I read, and even then sporadically because something within me begged for a chance to be heard, and although it scared me, I listened.

What is the truth?

Each day brought me another tiny sliver of peace, for each moment without a coping mechanism to carry me through created more space in my head for clarity and understanding. But it was slow going, a process that many times felt painful and boring and frustrating. *Please, God. Please, God. Please, God.* I had hoped for a revelation, for a lightning bolt to strike me and provide me with the answers that would stop my racing thoughts and heart palpitations, eliminate the sadness and guilt, but having always been so afraid to be anything less than perfect, it took me a fair amount of time to actually allow my emotions to surface and exist freely and without judgment, without *Don't be sad. Don't be mad. Don't be angry. Don't be frustrated. Don't be worried. Don't be.*

I went home to visit Mami and Papi one Sunday afternoon, for as much as I needed space for myself, they had always been my anchors, the two people who'd kept me tethered to reality, had kept me from drifting too far away.

When I walked in the door, I was hit with the smell of home, a combination of *sofrito, cafecito,* and Old Spice. I could see Papi through the sliding glass doors, his belly protruding through his shirt as he stood in front of the grill flipping the chicken breasts he'd seasoned with Mojo sauce, a cigarette dangling from his mouth and a glass of *"Yohnny Wocker en las rocas"* in one hand. Mami was moving around the small kitchen, singing a song under her breath as she prepared the rice, beans, and *platanos maduros.* I kissed her on the cheek and offered to help, knowing full well that Mami hated when other people got in her way. I sat down at the kitchen counter, recognizing immediately how different it was to sip on a glass of water instead of red wine.

Mami placed a salad in the middle of the kitchen counter, a blend of chopped romaine, sliced tomatoes, and red onions topped with olive oil on which I could not focus, my eyes instead drawn to a plate of leftover *chicharrones.* My mouth watered at the sight of the fried pork belly. She pulled a pack of corn tortillas out of the fridge, as no meal was ever complete unless she had her own personal staple. "No worry, *mija*," she said, as she dropped a few tortillas in a hot pan on the stove, "I made you salad *porque* I know how much you like your *vegetales.*"

I smiled, relieved that the sight of fried pork belly no longer came with a heaping side of anxiety. "Thanks, Mami, that looks delicious."

"*Oye mija*, and how are you? *¿Cómo te sientes?*"

My knee-jerk reaction was to say, "I'm fine, Mami. I'm good."

And maybe it was something in my voice, or maybe Mami had one of her *feelings*, because she grabbed a few pieces of pork belly, placed them in a tortilla, and topped them with salsa verde, her mood pensive and her eyes boring a hole into me as she leaned forward on the kitchen counter and said, "Are you sure? *Dime la verdad.*"

La verdad, I thought, as I watched her take a bite of her delicious pork belly taco.

In my mind, I reviewed the last few months, paused for a second to reflect on what I'd learned. I recalled how my heartbeat had slowed once I'd realized *la verdad* had changed the course of my life, when at fourteen years old I'd broken from the expectation that I become a concert pianist; how my thoughts had stopped racing once I'd realized *la verdad* had led me to England and Norway and Morocco and Croatia, for if I'd told Werner and Victor that I was going to law school or graduate school, I may not have received an invitation to a different life; how I'd allowed the tears to flow judgment-free once I'd understood that *la verdad* had literally saved my life, for without that phone call to Raz in the middle of the night, perhaps I would've done the unthinkable; how my heart had swelled with pride to know that *la verdad* had encouraged me to take bold risks and leave comfortable jobs, for in spite of the terrible habits and self-harming behaviors, deep down I had never stopped believing that sooner or later I would stumble upon what life wanted from me.

Still, I couldn't deny that *la verdad* had never been easy for me to accept. Never having been taught how to confidently be my own person or to sit with unpleasant emotions, I hadn't learned that being overweight was not a crime and that perfection was not a realistic ideal, hadn't understood that it was okay to walk a path different from what was expected, had never believed that I was *enough.* I'd never been able to grab ahold of the truth because the raging conflict between *who I am* and *who I think I should be* had long been provoking fear and insecurity and anxiety—all of which had triggered drinking and smoking and bingeing and purging.

Mami stood in front of me, imploring me to tell her *la verdad.* Papi walked inside as I contemplated what to say, the genuine concern in Mami's eyes and the sight of Papi's calloused hands helping me land on the most profound truth of all: that my parents had spent their entire lives swallowing their own truths each and every day, the hours they'd spent working tirelessly to provide for us not having left them with the time or wherewithal to consider their own grief and sadness and fears, this being another dimension to their *sacrificios* that I'd never considered. And rather than avoid and deflect and pretend and lie, I decided for once to honor their sacrifices in the most meaningful of ways by saying what was actually true for me, this special moment forever engraved in my heart as I recalled the words of *Abuela Meche*: "Someday you will know what this life wants from you."

I cleared my throat. "*¿La verdad?* I'm not feeling one-hundred percent, but I'm getting better."

"*¿Y eso?*" Mami said. "Are you depress-ed?"

I laughed at her pronunciation of the word and said, "No, Mami, I'm not depress-ed, just a little sad and worried sometimes."

"*Pero* why? Did something happen?"

"A whole fucking lifetime of bullshit happened," I wanted to say, but I didn't, the why and the how and the when and the what remarkably irrelevant as I rolled my own pork belly taco, a sense of relief and inner peace overwhelming me as I took a bite and relished the wonderful flavors of my two cultures, every part of me embracing truth as I shared openly my feelings and worries and even my history of heart palpitations, racing thoughts, and sweaty palms, Mami then leaning across the table to grab my hand and say, "*Ay mija,* me, too. I understand you."

And Papi, forever uncomfortable with Hallmark moments, gave me a look I'll never forget, a look that told me he, too, had had his fair share of hurt and suffering—all of it trapped somewhere beneath the cultural expectations he'd had no choice but to accept as a hot-blooded and determined *Cubano*, emotions that I glimpsed in his eyes for a brief moment before he winked and said, "*Oye, todo tiene solución.*"

And he was right.

EPILOGUE

"THANK YOU SO MUCH FOR YOUR TIME." I SAT DOWN IN a comfortable chair across from the Dean of Admissions at the Boston College School of Social Work.

He smiled warmly, instantly making me comfortable. "I'm glad you could make it. So, you're interested in the graduate program here at BC, is that right?"

"I am," I said, "very much so. I was hoping you could give me more information on the program and the requirements."

"Of course, my pleasure. Are you familiar at all with the field?"

Tell the truth, Yvonne. "No, not really. I've been working in the fitness industry for the past eleven years."

I smiled, proud of my accomplishments in the fitness industry since obtaining my PT certification in 2005. I'd worked with Equinox Fitness for five amazing years during which I'd been promoted to Personal Training Manager, a job that had taught me a great deal about running a business, valuable knowledge that I'd carried with me as I pursued a Fitness Manager job with Sports Club L.A., a company that had eventually moved me to Boston, where my knowledge and people skills had been put to the test as General Manager of the company's flagship health club. Three years, many great friends and memorable experiences later, I'd transitioned to Healthworks Fitness, a health club company dedicated to all things women and one that had given me the space and flexibility to simultaneously pursue a life coach certification.

Both my career and my spiritual growth had evolved

in a parallel fashion and in much the same way that one peels an onion; with each layer I'd peeled, I had discovered a new dimension to myself that had piqued my curiosity even further. From the very beginning of my career in the fitness industry, I had wanted to understand what drove the behavior of my training clients and then my staff, and more importantly, what environmental and societal factors drove my own. With this thirst, I'd enrolled in yoga teacher training early on in my career, and this *end of suffering* practice had helped me foster a greater awareness of myself and had helped me discover a deeper level of peace and understanding. It had taught me more about *being still*, about sitting in each moment and resting with the knowledge that regardless of what awaited me in the next moment, I would be okay, each moment would arrive and with it an opportunity to learn and grow.

Still, I hadn't been able to ignore the emotional and mental roadblocks around which I would never get simply because I lacked knowledge and education, obstacles that had continued to get in the way of understanding myself and the people I trained and with whom I worked. I'd peeled another layer of the onion by enrolling in a life coach certification in the hopes that I'd gain more valuable knowledge and insight into human behavior. I'd found the training and the process of becoming a life coach of tremendous value, but I hadn't been able to ignore that life coaching was largely a white person first-world luxury, applicable only to a select group of people with whom I did not feel a real connection. I had learned a great deal about myself and others by working in the fitness industry, but time and again I'd found myself questioning my career, wondering if perhaps there was another way in which I could be of service to others, these thoughts often drifting to the Latino population, to families like mine who might benefit from knowing themselves better and in turn be able to understand their first generation American children, this desire then prompting a conversation with a good friend, who had been curious to know why I'd never thought to become a mental health clinician.

We had been sitting on the back deck of the house I shared with my wonderful husband, a Colombian man who had fallen in love not only with my strength and confidence, but also with the cranky, irritable, funny, sweet, generous, hard-working, passionate, frustrated, annoyed, determined, sad, and scared Yvonne—all of me having shown up on our first date because I'd stumbled upon a sacred truth years before as I'd sat and cried alone in my apartment, it being that there was strength and peace to be found in vulnerability, incredible power in facing what is most uncomfortable and running toward it, not away, just as Mami had predicted when I'd flown out of her womb.

After our conversation, I had researched everything there was to know about becoming a mental health clinician, and I'd found a Latino Leadership Initiative program at Boston College. At forty-five years old, the thought of taking out student loans had in no way been a deterrent when I'd picked up the phone and made an appointment with the Dean of Admissions, my determination to help Latino families the sole reason I was sitting across from a stranger in an office of a college campus that reminded me of *Harry Potter*.

"You've been working in the fitness industry?" he said. "I'm sure you've had some interesting experiences."

You have no idea, I thought. "Yes, I certainly have. It's been very rewarding, and I've learned a great deal, but I want to pursue a career in mental health, and more specifically, to work with the Latino population. I understand a master's degree in Social Work is one way I can make this whole situation happen, is that correct?"

He laughed openly. "Yes, that is correct. The field of social work is quite expansive, but it sounds like you've narrowed it down to mental health within the Latino population. But tell me," he said, as he leaned forward in his chair, his arms resting on the desk, "what makes you want to work in mental health?"

A career in mental health was no trivial endeavor. For several days leading up to my meeting with the dean, I'd asked myself the same question, the answer requiring that I exlore my own challenges with mental health.

Many times over the years I'd been asked, "How did you recover from an eating disorder? What did you do? How did you go from drinking every single night to having a drink once in a while?" For as much as I'd wanted to give people a "Do this and do that" prescription, it had always been impossible for me to give them a straight answer. Overcoming an eating disorder, exercise addiction, and alcohol abuse had not all been a straight path, nor had it been an overnight phenomenon. Rather, it had been a slow, gradual shift in perspective that had begun when I'd sat on my couch and embarked on a quest to liberate myself from everything that had enslaved me for most of my life.

Instinctively I'd known that the road to recovery would entail more than just behavioral changes. I'd sensed that there had always been a core issue, something that had consistenly led me astray, the first shift in my perspective thus sparked by the realization that it had always been fear. I'd been afraid of not fitting in, of not being accepted, afraid of the unknown future, afraid of being weak, afraid of failing—the behaviors I'd used to cope with these fears nothing but Band-Aids for a deep, open wound for which the cure had ultimately been the "Triple A" Remedy: awareness, acceptance, and appreciation.

Awareness of these irrational fears had made it possible for me to challenge them. *Why am I afraid of the future? When have things not worked out? What, exactly, does it mean to belong? Will I die if I don't have a perfect body? Do I really need a man in my life to feel validated and whole?* The answers had come slowly but surely, and they'd helped me develop self-acceptance, which had paved the way for a new relationship with the me from whom I'd disconnected when I'd first stuck two fingers down my throat. *I like that I have compassion and empathy for others, that I value respect and truth, that I believe there is goodness in everyone, that I hold space for people and validate them.* Appreciation for myself as a human with both strengths and weaknesses had helped to free me from the self-defeating thoughts that had always held me hostage, and their absence had created space for whatever my physical body wanted me to know. *I don't want to work out for three hours. I just want to take a walk. I want to eat ice cream. Do yoga. Rest. Sleep.*

That's not to say that I hadn't continued to experience periods of anxiety or stress or difficult emotions, because even though I'd made a bold decision to resist using coping strategies to avoid intense discomfort, it certainly hadn't made me any less human or my life immune to trials and tribulations. But rather than regard them through the lens of fear, I'd learned to stand firm and approach them from a position of faith in God, who'd blessed me not with an easy way out of the storm, but with the strength to ride it out, to *be still, and know,* from Psalm 46:10. I'd learned to trust Him, to believe that into each moment I would arrive not in spite of the challenges I'd faced, but *because* of them, and that with truth as my compass, I would never feel lost.

My recovery had been unique to my circumstances; that I had been able to develop insight and perspective had been a product of the security and safety that my parents had worked so hard to provide; never had I suffered from hunger, poverty, or homelessness, and I'd never had to leave my home country in the hopes that I would find refuge and a better life in another country, hence my desire to serve the immigrant Latino population. I appreciated and loved my culture of origin, but I'd also recognized that within my community, mental health challenges are not openly discussed or explored, as too often the social and cultural stigma attached to mental illness acts as a major barrier for anyone who might be seeking help. That my parents had never been able to express their own emotions had troubled me, had made me wonder what Latino families would look like if they were given the permission to explore themselves and experience their emotions around a person from their same culture, if they were given an opportunity to develop their own perspectives and foster an even greater level of resilience with someone who understood their language and their beliefs. The thought of being able to accompany others on their journey had ignited a raging fire in my belly, an indicator to me that perhaps I'd finally connected to a greater purpose.

That I woke up one day and realized the path down which I'd been traveling my whole life had been preparing me all along for a greater purpose was proof of God's sense of humor. I smiled at the dean, his eyes curious as he patiently waited for an answer, the imaginary sound of God laughing in my ears as I said, "Why do I want to work in mental health? Well, it's quite a long story, but let's just say it was always meant to be."

ACKNOWLEDGMENTS

THE IDEA FOR THIS BOOK BEGAN AS A TINY SEED, AND I could not have watched it grow had it not been for the generous time and feedback provided by my friends and family: Miranda Hersey, Chris Schiefen, Adrian and Espy Saavedra, Rachel Lampke, Jorge Hernandez, and Annette Mooney. Thank you for every ounce of energy you devoted to this project. Blue Stiley, thank you for your example of perseverance; you remind me constantly that dreams are worth chasing.

Rose Granato, my sister from another mister, I don't know that I can properly articulate just how much I appreciate your time and friendship. Thank you for reading every single word from start to finish, and for the encouragement. You gave me that final push when quite frankly I was ready to trash the whole damn thing and get on with my life. You are a gift to the world and a blessing to mine.

Jeffrey Goldman at Santa Monica Press, thank you for taking more than just a peek at my project and for believing in its potential. You have made the stress and frustration of the past five years completely worth it!

Lisa Rojany, the editor who endeavored to correct my grammar and keep my run-on sentences in check, thank you for taking on this project. I am beyond honored that you lent your expertise to this book.

Adriana Senior and Jessica Ballardo, thank you for your incredibly valuable editorial input, and for your efforts in making sure this story flowed in all the right ways.

Charles Kazarian and Marcia Mavrides, thank you for not once doubting me and for your unconditional support and friendship.

Victor Lee, for being an example to me of hard work, dedication and perseverance. You are and always will be an inspiration to me.

Smaiyra Million, for seeing in me what I could not see, and for challenging me to rise. I am forever grateful and will cherish you always.

Todd Nordstrom, Lisa Brown and family, for your unrestricted friendship and fierce way of loving. I am beyond blessed to know you.

Danny Rosenberg, for doing what was never asked of you, and for returning to my life.

The Borrero/Grasso family, thank you for accepting me from day one, for welcoming me into your beautiful family and for showing me respect and kindness.

My brother Raul Coronado, and my "west side" family, thank you for never giving up on the search for us, for picking up the phone and making that phone call. My world has grown in a million ways since we connected, and your encouragement from so far away has been key to writing this book.

Abuela Meche, at one hundred years old, you continue to amaze and inspire me. Thank you, always, for loving me, and for showing me the way, time and again. And to my entire family in Mexico/California, thank you for letting me love you.

My Cuban *familia*, I am so proud to know you and to be part of this warm, crazy family. Thank you for loving me. Your honesty challenged me to accept people for who they are, and not for who I'd like them to be, and for that I am eternally grateful.

Julian Borrero, there are no words to express how

grateful I am for the freedom to show up in each moment, stressed, happy, grumpy, and most of all, in love with you. Thank you not so much for giving me the space, but for sharing it.

Thank you to my brother Raz, who has been with me from day one. Near or far, you will always be a force in my life, an anchor that tethers me to our childhood and to every moment of joy, sadness, fear, anger, happiness, and grief that we shared. I love you.

Mami, I have no words. That I am physically here on earth, and able to pursue every single dream that crosses my path is testament to every drop of sweat that fell from your forehead. I love you, Mami, now and always.

Papi, you may not be physically here, but your essence guides me every moment of the day. May you forever rest in peace and know that your legacy has made possible every word of this book. I love you, *mi viejo*.

Lastly, I could not have done this without the unconditional and relentless love of God, who has repeatedly pushed back on my understanding of what I deserve by bestowing on me His grace.

"I can do all things through Christ who strengthens me."
—Philippians 4:13

RESOURCES

SAMHSA's National Helpline (English and Spanish)
1-800-662-HELP
https://www.samhsa.gov/find-help/national-helpline

National Suicide Prevention Lifeline (English and Spanish)
1-800-273-TALK
https://suicidepreventionlifeline.org/

Crisis Text Line
Text HOME to 741741
https://www.crisistextline.org/

National Eating Disorder Helpline (NEDA)
1-800-931-2237 (translation services available on the phone)
https://www.nationaleatingdisorders.org/help-support/
contact-helpline

National Association of Anorexia Nervosa and Associated Disorders
1-888-375-7767
https://anad.org/get-help/eating-disorders-helpline/

Overeaters Anonymous
1-505-891-2664
https://oa.org/find-a-meeting/?type=0

National Hopeline Network
1-800-442-HOPE

Domestic Abuse and Violence Support
1-800-799-7233
www.thehotline.org

ABOUT THE AUTHOR

BORN IN LOS ANGELES to Mexican and Cuban parents, Castañeda was raised in Miami, where she eventually earned a BA in International Relations from Florida International University. She has worked in the restaurant, cruise line, education and hotel industry, and was contracted as a linguist with the Department of Justice. Having suffered from Bulimia Nervosa for over 15 years, Castañeda developed a passion for fitness and later pursued a career in the fitness industry, in which she worked as a Personal Trainer and General Manager for over ten years.

Currently, Castañeda is a Licensed Psychotherapist in Massachusetts (LICSW) and an Adjunct Professor of Boston College Graduate School of Social Work and Online Facilitator of BC School of Theology and Ministry. Aside from her own lived experiences, Castañeda has worked extensively with the underserved Hispanic/Latino population as a behavioral health clinician.

Castañeda is an iPEC Certified Life Coach, a Registered Yoga Teacher, a Corrective Exercise Specialist, a Kettlebell Coach and a 2nd Dan Black Belt in Shotokan Karate.